HERMETIC MAGIC

Here is . . . the Enochian Magic as taught by the Hermetic Order of the Golden Dawn, but in a complete and easy-to-read textbook that can be used by the magical novice.

Here is . . . a dictionary of Enochian words listed in order of gematria value to facilitate the magical process.

Here is . . . basic information of correspondence and original ideas to also please the seasoned magician.

In late sixteenth-century England Dr. John Dee, Astrologer Royal to Queen Elizabeth I, began working with his assistant Edward Kelly, setting down a magical alphabet and system that was presented to him by extraterrestrial intelligences. Communication was by "skrying," or crystal-gazing. The system was unique. It was embellished by Dee's own Qabalistic speculations and by further magical material dictated by the spirits. The Enochian alphabet is unrelated to any previous lettering system. It is almost a series of Qabalistic pictographs meant to be imagined visually and not commonly inscribed. The Enochian language has a unique grammar and syntax structure. Over the years since its introduction, it has come to be regarded as a "classic" of magical working. It was adopted and refined by the Hermetic Order of the Golden Dawn and, later, by Aleister Crowley.

In this book you are led carefully along the path from "A Brief History of the Enochian Magical System," through "How to Speak Enochian," "How to Invoke," "The Calls," "Egyptian Deities" and "Chief Hazards" to "How to Visit the Aethyrs in Spirit Vision (Astral Projection)." Not a step is missed; not a necessary instruction forgotten.

We are "more than human. The human is but one expression of the divine, albeit an enormously important one. Every magician who has experienced the higher Aethyrs is aware of the awesome power of the magically directed will. S/he is also fully aware of the karmic consequences of his/her thoughts and actions." So say the authors.

You must set foot upon the path with as true a map of the way ahead as it is possible to obtain. And this book is such a map. Take it and move forward.

About the Authors

Gerald J. Schueler, born in Darby, Pennsylvania, and his wife, Betty Sherlin Schueler, born in Washington DC, currently reside in Maryland. Jerry is a systems analyst, free-lance writer, editor and artist. Betty is a computer consultant, free-lance writer, editor and artist. The Schuelers have co-authored many articles on anthropology, computers, dogs, philosophy, magick, and other subjects.

To Write to the Authors

If you wish to contact the authors or would like more information about this book, please write to the authors in care of Llewellyn Worldwide, and we will forward you request. The authors and the publisher appreciate hearing from you and learning of your enjoyment of this book and how it has helped you. Llewellyn Worldwide cannot guarantee that every letter written to the authors can be answered, but all will be forwarded. Please write to:

Gerald and Betty Schueler
c/o Llewellyn Worldwide
P.O. Box 64383-710, St. Paul, MN 55164-0383, U.S.A.

Please enclose a self-addressed, stamped envelope for reply, or $1.00 to cover costs. If outside the U.S.A., enclose international postal reply coupon.

Free Catalog from Llewellyn

For more than 90 years Llewellyn has brought its readers knowledge in the fields of metaphysics and human potential. Learn about the newest books in spiritual guidance, natural healing, astrology, occult philosophy and more. Enjoy book reviews, new age articles, a calendar of events, plus current advertised products and services. To get your free copy of *Llewellyn's New Worlds of Mind and Spirit*, send your name and address to:

Llewellyn's New Worlds of Mind and Spirit
P.O. Box 64383-710, St. Paul, MN 55164-0383, U.S.A.

ABOUT LLEWELLYN'S HIGH MAGICK SERIES

Practical Magick is performed with the aid of ordinary, everyday implements, is concerned with the things of the Earth and the harmony of Nature, and is considered to be the magick of the common people. *High Magick*, on the other hand, has long been considered the prerogative of the affluent and the learned. Some aspects of it certainly call for items expensive to procure and for knowledge of ancient languages and tongues, though that is not true of all High Magick. There was a time when, to practice High Magick, it was necessary to apprentice oneself to a Master Magician, or *Mage*, and to spend many years studying and practicing.

High Magick is the transformation of the Self to the Higher Self. Some aspects of it also consist of rites designed to conjure spirits, or entities, capable of doing one's bidding. Motive is the driving force of these magicks and is critical for success.

In recent years there has been a change from the traditional thoughts regarding High Magick. The average intelligence today is vastly superior to that of four or five centuries ago. Minds attuned to computers are finding a fascination with the mechanics of High Magical conjurations (this is especially true of the mechanics of Enochian Magick).

The Llewellyn High Magick Series has taken the place of the Mage, the Master Magician who would teach the apprentice. "Magick" is simply making happen what one desires to happen—as Aleister Crowley put it: "The art, or science, of causing change to occur in conformity with will." The Llewellyn High Magick Series shows how to effect that change and details the steps necessary to cause it.

Magick is a tool. High Magick is a potent tool. Learn to use it. Learn to put it to work to improve your life. This series will help you do just that.

Also by Gerald and Betty Schueler

An Advanced Guide to Enochian Magick
Enochian Physics
Egyptian Magick
Enochian Tarot
Enochian Yoga
The Enochian Workbook

Computer Software

The Electric Tarot
Magical Diary
Tree of Life
Enochian Magic
    Enochian Alphabet
    Enochian Gematria
    Watchtower Tables
    Tablet of Union
    The Thirty Aethyrs
    Kings and Seniors

Enochian Magic
A Practical Manual

by Gerald and Betty Schueler

1996
Llewellyn Publications
St. Paul, Minnesota 55164-0383, U.S.A.

FIRST EDITION, 1984
SECOND EDITION, 1985
THIRD EDITION, 1990
Third Printing, 1996

Interior artwork by Bill Fugate
Cover art by Michael Kucharski
Cover design by Tom Grewe

Library of Congress Cataloging-in-Publication Data
Schueler, Gerald J., 1942-
    Enochian magic.

    (Llewellyn's high magick series)
    1. Magic. I. Title. II. Series.
BF1611.S38   1985   133.4'3   84-48087
ISBN 0-87542-710-3

Llewellyn Publications
A Division of Llewellyn Worldwide, Ltd.
P.O. 64383, St. Paul, MN 55164-0383

CONTENTS

TABLES

Note: Grateful acknowledgement is given to the following books, from
   which some of the illustrations in this present work are taken.
   The Golden Dawn by Israel Regardie
   Book IV by Aleister Crowley
   The Equinox (vols I—VII) by Aleister Crowley

The Objectives of this Manual

This manual is an attempt to eliminate the unnecessary complexity of the Enochian magical system, while combining its numerous elements into a single source. The system described here borrows heavily from both the Golden Dawn and Aleister Crowley. The earnest student is advised to study *The Golden Dawn* (St. Paul, MN: Llewellyn Publications), by Israel Regardie, especially Volume IV. Also recommended are Crowley's *The Vision and the Voice* and *Liber LXXXIX Vel Chanokh*, both of which can be found in *Gems of the Equinox* by Israel Regardie.

This manual contains the complete theory behind the system, with explanations and tabulated data, together with step-by-step instructions and detailed examples for the serious student. Charts and tables are provided to summarize data which are unavailable elsewhere. Any student willing to spend time and effort will have a corresponding degree of success. The truly amazing thing about this system is that it really does work.

1989 was the fifth anniversary of the publication of *Enochian Magic*. My wife, Betty, and I thought that this would be an appropriate time to update the material contained in the first edition. When this book was first published, producing it was a cumbersome proposition. By today's standards, everything had to be done manually. As a result, the first edition of the book contained many mistakes. It is our hope that those mistakes will be corrected in this edition.

The publication of *Enochian Magic* precipitated a rebirth of interest in the Enochian magical system. As a result, many new books have come out on the subject, and many more are in the planning stages. With so many books to choose from, we hope that you will find this book worthy of space on your library shelf.

—Gerald J. Schueler

1

TABLE I. THE ENOCHIAN ALPHABET, WITH TITLES AND ENGLISH EQUIVALENTS

Enochian	Title	English
𝋌	Un	A.
✔	Pe	B.
13	Veh	C or K.
𝋌	Gal	D.
𝋌	Graph	E.
𝋌	Orth	F.
𝋌	Ged	G.
𝋌	Na-hath	H.
𝋌	Gon	I, Y, or J.
𝋌	Ur	L.
𝋌	Tal	M.
𝋌	Drun	N.
𝋌	Med	O.
𝋌	Mals	P.
𝋌	Ger	Q.
𝋌	Don	R.
𝋌	Fam	S.
𝋌	Gisa	T.
𝋌	Vau	U, V, W.
𝋌	Pal	X.
𝋌	Ceph	Z.

A BRIEF HISTORY OF
THE ENOCHIAN MAGICAL SYSTEM

As far as anyone knows, Enochian Magic was first introduced to modern man by John Dee and Edward Kelly (sometimes spelled Kelley). Working together, these two men rediscovered an ancient form of powerful magic which had been lost in the mists of antiquity.

John Dee was born in England in 1527, in the small village of Mortlake, on the Thames near London. It was the Renaissance, a "new age" of enlightenment and reformation. Magic and science had not yet separated. Mathematics was considered somewhat of a black art, and was widely feared by the populace. The use of symbols such as the plus and minus signs was just beginning. This was the world upon which John Dee would leave an indelible mark as a philosopher, mathematician, geographer, technologist, antiquarian, and magician.

Dee entered college at the age of 15 and was an outstanding student. At only 23 years of age he was a "learned man" much sought after by king, queen, and emperor alike. His family's property, in Mortlake, was a center for science and learning, and housed one of the finest libraries in all of Europe, if not the world. Queen Elizabeth I of England made him a Royal Astrologer, but he served his queen in a much wider capacity. Throughout her long reign, Elizabeth depended upon John Dee for advice on everything from politics to magic. In his role of general royal confidante, Dee helped shape the new world which was emerging from a cloistered past. He was a beacon of light in Europe's new dawn of reason.

Edward Kelly was almost the exact antithesis of John Dee. Where Dee was intelligent, curious, honest, and kind, Edward Kelly appears to have been somewhat of a rogue, starting from the time he was old enough for others to take notice of his duplicity. Born at Worcester in 1555, Kelly attended Oxford under the name of Edward Talbot. While at Oxford, he participated in some sort of mischief and had to leave suddenly. He was pilloried in Lancaster for forgery a few years later. He acquired his knowledge of the occult from Thomas Allen, a magus like Dee. Unfortunately, Kelly never learned to use this knowledge for the betterment of mankind.

Dee and Kelly first became associated when Kelly visited Dee's home in 1582. He immediately ingratiated himself to Dee by seeing visions in Dee's crystal. Dee and Kelly formed a close association which lasted for seven years. Together, they produced a staggering amount of original work in the fields of occultism and magic.

By using a collection of different crystals, or shewstones, Kelly was able to communicate with extraterrestrial intelligences, or angels. Dee directed the ceremonies, observed the proceedings, and carefully wrote down the results of each session. In this way the Enochian magical system was revealed to modern man.

In 1583, Dee and Kelly left England to tour Europe. Supposedly, they were studying the Qabalah and skrying, (see page 102), but some historians believe the two were actually acting as spies for Elizabeth, and that their magical activities were simply a cover. Whichever was the case, much work was accomplished during their travels on the continent.

In 1589, Dee returned to England after an abrupt parting with Kelly. He returned to his old role at the court, but his influence was beginning to wane. Soon, Dee's friends were either dead or out of power and he was without money. The ascension in 1603 of King James I, who feared magic and had no love for Dee, assured Dee's ultimate downfall. He died penniless in 1608.

As for Kelly, he remained on the Continent and was

knighted by Rudolph II for his alchemical efforts. A scoundrel to the end, he died from injuries incurred while trying to escape from prison in 1595. It is claimed that Kelly's occupation as a medium ended the day he was skrying the seventh Aethyr and received a message that terrified him so completely that he vowed never to skry again. This is the message which so frightened Kelly, and brought an end to Dee's and Kelly's preoccupation with Enochian Magic:

"I am the daughter of Fortitude and ravished every hour from my youth. For behold, I am Understanding, and science dwelleth in me; and the heavens oppress me. They cover and desire me with infinite appetite; for none that are earthly have embraced me, for I am shadowed with the Circle of the Stars, and covered with the morning clouds. My feet are swifter than the winds, and my hands are sweeter than the morning dew. My garments are from the beginning, and my dwelling place is in myself. The Lion knoweth not where I walk, neither do the beasts of the field understand me. I am deflowered, yet a virgin; I sanctify and am not sanctified. Happy is he that embraceth me: for in the night season I am sweet, and in the day full of pleasure. My company is a harmony of many symbols, and my lips sweeter than health itself. I am a harlot for such as ravish me, and a virgin with such as know me not. Purge your streets, O ye sons of men, and wash your houses clean; make yourselves holy, and put on righteousness. Cast out your old strumpets, and burn their clothes and then I will bring forth children unto you and they shall be the Sons of Comfort in the Age that is to come."

In 1887, in England, a group of mysterious and highly secret adepts formed a brotherhood known as the Hermetic Order of the Golden Dawn. The group was led by three imgainative magicians—Samuel Liddell Mathers, William Wynn Westcott, and Dr. William R. Woodman. At first, the group consisted of intellectuals, artists, and the clergy, but later, the group grew to include a broader spectrum, encompassing virtually every segment of society. Over the years, the Golden Dawn would include such prominent people as Yeats, Aleister Crowley, Dion Fortune, and A.E. Waite.

The Golden Dawn was able to maintain guarded secrecy of its system until one of its members, Aleister Crowley, published his own version of it, and then left that Order to form his own. When that group failed to flourish, he accepted an invitation to join, and head, another group—the O.T.O., or *Ordo Templi Orientis.* Crowley claimed to have been Kelly in a past life. This was the reason he gave for his uncanny ability to skry. His experiences were recorded in a book called *The Vision and the Voice,* which was written in such obscure symbolism and technical language that few today can understand it. Crowley, whose colorful life suggests elements of the rogue, was an amazing psychic and a prolific writer and poet. He advanced the Enochian system by revealing those planetary and numerical correspondences which make Enochian gematria possible.

The published works of Crowley and the Golden Dawn differ slightly in spellings and in certain correspondences. There is also a marked difference in emphasis on certain teachings. In this book, we have tried to blend the best of thse two groups, the Golden Dawn and the O.T.O., and we have further refined, expanded, and modernized the system of Enochian Magic to make it more synchronized with today's highly technological world. To do this, we have had to take liberties with some of the original structure. The results meld the highly fragmented, convoluted teachings and practices of Enochian Magic into a streamlined, efficient system which can be used by anyone wishing to learn more about the wonders of the Magical Universe.

The Enochian Alphabet—

The magical language which Dee and Kelly revealed was so powerful that they had to spell names backwards to prevent conjuring unwanted demons. They believed the simple pronouncing of a demon's name was sufficient to bring that demon forth into manifestation. They called their language *Enochian* after the biblical patriarch Enoch, who is said to have "walked with God." Enoch was also the name of an ancient group of Adepts who kept the flame of occultism burning through the dark ages. Table 1 shows the Enochian alphabet, with its titles for each letter of the alphabet, along with their English equivalents as taught by the Golden Dawn.

Alphabet Numerical Values

Each letter of the Enochian alphabet corresponds with planetary, elemental, or Tarot properties. In addition, each has a numerical value so that a workable gematria for the alphabet can be used, as shown in Table II. By substituting numbers for letters, we can add up the numerical equivalents for words and names. Words that are numerically equal have hidden or "occult" correspondences. In this way, an entire Enochian Qabalah, like the Jewish and Greek Qabalahs, can be derived.

The Angelic Secret Language

The Golden Dawn taught that the alphabet was an ancient language, traces of which could be found in the sacred and secret mysteries of some of the oldest religions in the world. Parts of it are found on rock-cut pillars and on the remains of ancient temples. However, it is doubtful if it was ever spoken. Enochian was probably used more as a system of sigils and glyphs to record and give life to important ideas.

The question of how Dee and Kelly came upon this language has never been satisfactorily answered. According to Dee's diary, Kelly looked through a shewstone and saw an angel pointing, in succession, to letters that were prepared in rows and columns on well over one hundred different tablets. Kelly told Dee which letter was being indicated by the angel, and Dee wrote it down. He was always careful to give the row and column number, fearing to say the letter aloud. Magical seals and talismans were devised with Enochian letters on them. The 30 Aethyrs, or planes, were described, and the names of the angelic hierarchies of the magical Universe were carefully recorded. After each message was received, it was rewritten backwards. The angel himself dictated each letter in reverse order because of the power of the language.

If the angels who revealed the Enochian language knew the source of their language, they did not reveal it to Dee or Kelly. Because of this, the origins of the Enochian language will probably remain a mystery.

TABLE II. ALPHABETICAL CORRESPONDENCES AND GEMATRIA VALUES

English Equivalent	Planetary/ Element Correspondence	Tarot Correspondence	Gematria Value
A	Taurus	Hierophant	6
B	Aries	Star	5
C,K	Fire	Judgement/Aeon	300
D	Spirit	Empress	4
E	Virgo	Hermit	10
F	Cauda Draconis	Juggler	3
G	Cancer	Chariot	8
H	Air	Fool	1
I,J,Y	Sagittarius	Temperance/Art	60
L	Cancer	Chariot	8
M	Aquarius	Emperor	90
N	Scorpio	Death	50
O	Libra	Justice	30
P	Leo	Strength/Lust	9
Q	Water	Hanged Man	40
R	Pisces	Moon	100
S	Gemini	Lovers	7
T	Leo	Strength/Lust	9
	Caput Draconis	High Priestess	3
U,V,W	Capricorn	Devil	70
X	Earth	Universe	400
Z	Leo	Strength/Lust	9
	Caput Draconis	High Priestess	3

HOW THE MAGIC WORKS: THE WILL

Every intentional act is a magical act. It is the human intent or will that makes an act magical, nothing else. This is a very important idea. Most of our daily actions are actually magical. We are in fact, consciously or unconsciously, all magicians.

As one's intent makes an act magical, so it also colors that magic either black or white. As a general rule, *"black"* magic is any intentional act whose purpose is purely selfish or ego-oriented. By contrast, *"white"* magic is any intentional act whose motive is altruistic or non-ego-oriented.

The Enochian magical system comprises two chief types of magical operations: (i) invocations of the ruling spirits (*i.e.* bringing *them* to *you*) and (ii) astral traveling into the quadrants and Aethyrs described by the system (*i.e. you* going to *them*). Both types have been used effectively and can be used today by the willing student. The system works because the magician wills it so. On the other hand, the system will not work if such is one's will.

There can be a difference between "will" and "desire". The will exercises a strong determination toward conscious and deliberate action. Desire, on the other hand, can be whimsical or impulsive. It is the task of each student to carefully examine his mind and sort out the capricious desires from those strong determinations that mark the will. The quest for one's *TRUE WILL*, that for which one comes into this world, can take many years.

HOW THE MAGIC WORKS: THE MOTIVE

The motive is the driving force behind every magical act and is critical for success. Curiosity alone is usually not sufficient.

The student must look within himself to see what his true motive is. Is it selfish? Will a successful result benefit only himself? Will anyone be hurt? How these and similar questions are answered will determine the karma of the operation.

Karma is the cause and effect relationship that exists between all things and it operates on all planes of existence. Every magical act is charged with karma; physical, mental, emotional, and so on. Karma does not reward or punish. It is amoral. It is impersonal. It is ruthless. It continually seeks a balance between extremes and cares not for the ill-fated magician who inadvertently stresses its delicate network.

Religion and morality aside for a moment, any magical act that falls under the general heading of *white* magic will produce karmic effects that are pleasant, while acts that are *black* (*i.e.* selfish) will produce karmic effects that sooner or later are most unpleasant. This being the case, common sense dictates the choice of proper motive for the wise magician.

HOW THE MAGIC WORKS: THE PLANES

Central to Enochian magic, and all other forms of true magic, is the doctrine concerning the cosmic planes of existence. This doctrine says that divinity expresses itself downward (or outward) from spirit into matter in graduated steps—something like cosmic quanta. Each of these steps is a *plane* or universe. Our earth, and the entire physical cosmos, is on the seventh (*i.e.* lowest and most dense) of these cosmic planes.

TABLE III. THE SEVEN COSMIC PLANES
AND THEIR CORRESPONDING BODIES

Plane No.	Occult System	Qabalistic System	Enochian System Plane	Body
1	Divine	Three Planes	Divine	Divine Body
2	Upper Spirit'l (abstract spirit)	of the Divine		
		and Formless	Spiritual	Spiritual Body
3	Lower Spirit'l (concrete spirit)	World		
		THE GREAT OUTER ABYSS		
4	Upper Mental (abstract mind)	Archetypal		
			Mental	Mental Body
5	Lower Mental (concrete mind)	Intellectual (Creative)		
6	Astral	Substantial (Formative)	Astral	Astral Body
7	Physical	Physical	Physical	Physical Body

Table III shows the usual occult and Qabalistic divisions of these planes and the corresponding bodies that we assume on each. There is no need to create any of these bodies, we each already have them. What *is* needed is to learn to function consciously in them. Notice that the Abyss marks the major division between form and formlessness. Here the Oversoul, or Reincarnating Ego, takes on "new bodies" with each incarnation of the spirit. The doctrine of reincarnation is used to understand and describe these seven planes and how we function on them. This is because initiation into these planes is similar to death.

Enochian Magic views the cosmic planes as containing special regions, called Watchtowers. The four Watchtowers of Earth, Water, Air, and Fire surround our physical Earth, each on a different cosmic plane. Above these Watchtowers is a special region called the Tablet of Union, which is located on the spiritual plane above the Abyss.

The major difference between the leveled or stepped system of occultism shown in Table III and the Enochian is that in the latter these cosmic planes are considered as concentric spheres. The Enochian system subdivides these concentric spheres into thirty regions or zones which it calls the *Aethyrs*.

HOW TO SPEAK ENOCHIAN

The pronunciation of Enochian, as taught by both the Golden Dawn and Aleister Crowley, is similar to Hebrew. Ten major rules to remember are:

1. Most consonants have an *e* or *eh* added; for example, the letter B is pronounced *beh* and the letter K as *keh*.

2. Most vowels have an *h* added; for example, the letter A is pronounced *ah*.

3. The Enochian word SOBHA is pronounced in three syllables as *soh-beh-hah*. This is the general rule for words.

4. The letter G can be either hard as in the word *gimel* or soft as in *jimel*.

5. The letters Y and I are interchangable, as are the letters V and U. The letters *j* and *w* are seldom used.

6. The letter X can be like the *s* in *samekh*, or like the *tz* in *tzaddi*.

7. The letter S can be pronounced either as *ess* or *seh*.

8. The letter R can be pronounced either as *rah*, *reh*, or *ar*.

9. The letter Z is pronounced as *zod* or *Zeh*. It is interchangeable with the letter S.

10. The vowel I is pronounced as *ee*.

Examples of Name Pronouncements.
Correctly pronouncing the names of the gods, spirits, and rulers of the quadrants and Aethyrs, is critical in order to obtain satisfactory magical results. As a rule of thumb, the syllables should flow together easily and poetically—almost like a song. Seldom is a harsh or sharp sound made.

The reciting aloud of these names should be like speaking mantras; each should be intoned in one long flowing breath. As an example, recite the name of a

14

Senior of Air, HABIORO. This should be done in a single smooth breath. Say, *Hah-bee-oh-roh.* The mouth should make four distinct syllables with this name. During an invocation of this Senior, the magician must focus his mind on the qualities of HABIORO, while repeating his name in four melodious syllables.

Some names are subject to several possible spellings. This is because some squares on the Watchtowers contain multiple letters. As a general rule, pronunciation should include all letters, or the highest whenever only one is desired (the multiple letters are given like a fraction with a higher and a lower row). However, there are exceptions to this rule.

An example here is the name of the great King of Earth, IKZHIKAL. This name can also be spelled IKZHHHAL, IKZHIHAL, and IKZHHKAL because the squares give IKZH$^I_H$$^H_K$AL where the fifth and sixth letters are multiple. The best way of pronouncing this King's name is to choose the variant spelling that has the most meaningful gematric value. In this case, this is *Ee-keh-zod-hee-kal,* or *Ee-keh-zeh-hee-kal.*

How To Vibrate The Names.

In addition to pronunciation, some names should be vibrated. This is especially important during invocations. When a name is to be vibrated, the speaker must imagine the sound of the name going outward from himself into the farthest reaches of the universe. As the name is being pronounced verbally, it must be projected outward mentally. After verbal pronunciation, the magician should still be able to "hear" the name psychically and "see" the name expand over the Watchtowers and Aethyrs. The vibration of a name requires full concentration.

HOW THE MAGIC WORKS: THE IMAGINATION

Imagination is essential in magic. It is the golden key to the performance of any magical operation. All of the usual magic paraphernalia—incense, music, rituals, chants, robes, signs, symbols, and the like—are useful only insofar as they are able to stimulate the imagination.

For example, during an invocation of a spirit, while chanting the name, the magician must concentrate on the known qualities and characteristics until the spirit is clearly visualized in his mind. It is a mental image held by the magician. This image will stimulate the precipitation of the spirit. Because of this intense imagery, it is usually impossible to determine if a spirit actually manifested physically or not. It is a point of interest here that it doesn't matter in the least so far as the results are concerned.

This magical image is called a *telesmatic image* and it is important for effective results. Every Angel, King, Senior, Governor, and so forth, has his own telesmatic image. However, this telesmatic image can vary widely, within certain limits, with each magician. No Angel or King will appear exactly the same to every magician, though certain characteristics are universal. For example, every Angel in the Watchtower of Fire must exhibit a fiery nature in one way or another. Appearance, in every case, must correspond with locality and function.

The imagination is the creative faculty of man. With its use, thoughts take on form. This may not seem to be of concern on Earth, where thoughts have little effect, but in the psychic world, which one sees in the "Spirit Vision", it is very important indeed. There, thoughts are real things. On the Mental Plane the thought-form of a tree, for example, is as real to one's spirit vision as an oak is to one's eyes on the Physical Plane. The magical power of imagination to create thought forms is called *Kriya Sakti*. The conscious use of thought forms is possible because of Kriya Sakti. The conscious use of Kriya Sakti on Earth is rare and difficult to develop. But on the Astral and Mental Planes it is much easier. Actually, we all use Kriya Sakti subconsciously; it is the power which causes dreams. Its control is equivalent to being able to fall asleep and consciously direct a dream.

HOW THE MAGIC WORKS: THE SPIRITS

According to the Enochian magical system, the universe is chock full of spiritually intelligent beings and forces. Every region in space, throughout the seven cosmic planes, is ruled by a hierarchy of deities. Each has a slightly different character and quality. Which one we choose to encounter, depends upon our motive for the magical operation.

This idea is in accord with a basic tenet of occultism: the entire universe is alive. There is no such thing as dead matter (or dead anything else). However, because things have life (and therefore consciousness) completely foreign to ours, they appear quite lifeless and communication with them is impossible. A corollary of this tenet is that there is no such thing as empty space. Every mathematical point in space is a center of some kind of consciousness (called a *monad*). A *vacuum* is a figment of our imagination. We can detect nothing in a vacuum, but something is there nonetheless.

Are these spirits real? Do the Kings and Seniors have objective existence? Here the student must adopt a special attitude; it is more convenient to accept their existence than it is to reject it. If we accept them as real, the operations have satisfactory results; if we reject their reality, the magic will not work. It is just that simple. Belief is important in order to properly goad the imagination. Whether they actually exist or not (*i.e.* whether they exist objectively or subjectively) must be answered individually by each person according to his experiences and convictions.

HOW THE MAGIC WORKS: THE ROD

The magician will have to trace pentagrams and hexagrams during invocation and banishing rituals. With this in mind, a Rod or Wand of some kind is required. This Rod is the only magical implement that is actually required for Enochian Magic, although the four Elemental Weapons could certainly be used. These were described in some detail by the Golden Dawn and consecrated by appropriate rituals, but the following could be used just as well:

    The Fire Wand—This can be a dowel rod about ten inches long, painted red.

    The Water Cup—This can be any blue cup, either metal or glass.

    The Air Dagger—This can be a simple knife or letter-opener, painted bright yellow.

    The Earth Pantacle—This can be a round wooden disk about four inches in diameter and painted black.

The magic Rod can be a wooden dowel, either ¼- or ½-inch in diameter, and about one foot long. It should be painted gold or, if preferred, divided into equal sections of white, blue, yellow, black, and red, which are the colors of the elements. Painting or engraving the symbols of the elements is also encouraged.

The Wand symbolizes the highest will of the magician. This is the so-called *True Will;* an individual expression of the Great Work. It is the aim of macrocosmic human evolution as expressed in the microcosmic magician. This works best when it is unconscious and is allowed to influence the entire life and life-style of the magician as a matter of course. If the Great Work is likened to climbing a mountain, then the True Will is the individual pathway taken up the slopes to arrive at the common peak. The True Will is symbolized by the straightness and arrow-like nature of the Rod.

HOW THE MAGIC WORKS: THE GREAT WORK

The ultimate aim, and only truly worthy purpose of magic (like mysticism) is to awaken the consciousness of man to his inherent divinity, the god within. Everyone has an inner spiritual being. The mind and personality are but faint expressions of it. The physical body is its far-distant reflection. Table III (page 12) shows that each of man's vehicles is a creative expression of the other, from the spiritual down to the physical. However, few are directly aware of this and even fewer can focus consciousness on their spiritual body, as easily as they can on their physical body. Indeed, modern psychology shows that most people have a difficult time being aware of their own emotions and thoughts. The *subconscious* seems an alien and threatening land, ready to snuff out the ego at the first opportunity. If we are unable to focus consciousness on the astral body (emotions) or on the mental body (thoughts), how can we do so on the causal and spiritual bodies? How can we function in the spiritual body as consciously as we do in the physical body? It is not easy, yet this is exactly what the real magician tries to do. The attempt is called the "Great Work" and it is the toil of many lifetimes. Every magical operation worthy of being performed (i.e. white magic) is done to further this Great Work. Every invocation and all traveling in the Spirit Vision, as described in Enochian Magic, should be done solely to tread the path which continues, in some degree, the Great Work.

THE HOLY TABLE

Dee and Kelly devised a Holy Twelvefold Table containing seven different talismans, as shown in Figure 1. This table is covered with Enochian writings. In the center is:

O I T
M L U
L M L
O O E

Figure 1. The Holy Table

Reading across, we get OIT which means "this is"; MLU which means "a surge"; LML meaning "a treasure"; and OOE meaning "ecstasy." Taken together, this says, "This is an outpouring of rich ecstasy."

Reading downward we get OMLO which can mean "knowledge of the first"; ILMO meaning "of the Aethyrs"; and TULE meaning "also of the last." Taken together, this says, "The knowledge of the first of the Aethyrs even unto the last."

A detailed description of the thirty Aethyrs is given later, however the key to their understanding is contained here in this Holy Table.

Around the outer edge of the Holy Table are Enochian letters. These are arranged without any visible break or starting point. Reading the message, either clockwise or counterclockwise, is to no avail. The center four words give the key to reading this message. This is because the words OIT, MUL, LML, and OOE are all found in the surrounding message. The message's words are thus read clockwise beginning with the word OIT, but the letters within the words are read counterclockwise (*i.e.* backwards), except in a few instances where they are scrambled into an anagram. The message around the Holy Table can be translated as follows:

This is the place of the outpouring
  OIT   EOGA   MLU

of forgotten treasure in the form of ecstasy.
  LN-BAM   LML   EOAN   OOE

Only   Fire   is substantial here. This is
GZE PLG (PRG)   BASP   OI

   the way   of   Babalon and of
PSEA (ESAP) M OAVAANBBL (BABALON-V)

the Beast   who is   the First Form.
LN-NIA-O   SOB   SSNO (ZON)   L.
    The eyes only   need rest upon   the name of
EG (GE) OOEEON   F   G-DO
any   guardian   and its representative
    BNG (BRABZG)   SMAN-M

will speedily be encountered.
      MEL-F

This message mentions "Babalon" and the "Beast", a favorite theme of Aleister Crowley. According to these directions, a simple glance at the awesome name of a "guardian" will be sufficient to precipitate an encounter. The reader should take this as a dire warning. Although the likelihood of a physical manifestation of one of these guardians, right before the reader's eyes, is remote, a psychic manifestation in the form of an alien impulse or desire is highly probable. The danger here is that one may ignore this warning, being quite content that no ugly or mischievous Demon will suddenly appear before him in a puff of grey smoke. However, Demons come in other forms than those seen with eyes. The reader must guard his mind. That Dee and Kelly clearly believed this themselves is evidenced by the way they carefully anagramed the name of BABALON in the message, fearing that a straightforward spelling would bring her too close. History shows that Kelly himself finally became a victim to one of these strange and powerful Enochian forces.

THE HOLY PANTACLE

The Holy Pantacle, or Great Seal, devised by Dee and Kelly is shown in Figure 2. This magical device was carefully carved in wax and placed on top of the Holy Table during certain operations. The pantacle contains the sacred names of many great Angels.

Figure 2. The Holy Pantacle or Great Seal.

I. The seven great names of God, whose pronunciations are unknown, are:
    1. SAAI$^2_8{}^1$EME ($^2_8{}^1$ is probably "El")

24

2. BTZKASE[30]
3. HEIDENE
4. DEIMO[30]A
5. I[26]MEGCBE
6. ILAOI[2][8][1]VN
7. IHRIAAL[2][8][1]

II. Names of four groups of Angels can be found by reading the heptagram of the Pantacle obliquely:

A.
1. E *(Eh)*
2. Me *(Meh)*
3. Ese *(Es-seh)*
4. Iana *(Ee-ah-nah)*
5. Akele *(Ah-keh-leh)*
6. Azdobn *(Ah-zod-doh-ben)*
7. Stimcul *(Ess-tee-em-kul)*

B.
1. I *(Ee)* (Sol)
2. IH *(Ee-heh)* (Luna)
3. Ilr *(Ee-lar)* (Venus)
4. Dmal *(Dem-ah-el)* (Jupiter)
5. Heeoa *(Heh-oh-ah)* (Mars)
6. Beigia *(Beh-ee-gee-ah)* (Mercury)
7. Stimcul *(Ess-tee-em-kul)* (Saturn)

C.
1. S *(Ess)*
2. Ab *(Ab-beh)*
3. Ath *(Ah-teh)*
4. Ized *(Ee-zod-deh)*
5. Ekiei *(Eh-kee-ehee)*
6. Madimi *(Em-ah-dee-mee)*
7. Esemeli *(Ess-em-el-ee)*

D.
1. L *(El)*
2. Aw *(Ah-weh)*

3. Ave *(Ah-veh)*
4. Liba *(El-ee-bah)*
5. Iocle *(Ee-oh-keh-leh)*
6. Hagone *(Hah-goh-neh)*
7. Ilemese *(Ee-leh-meh-seh)*

III. Seven great Angels are named. These are the Angels of the Seven Circles of Heaven:
   1. SAB-ATH-IEL "He who is first in works"
   2. Z-EDEK-IEL "He who is first in attainment"
   3. MAD-IM-IEL "He who is first in expressing God"
   4. SE-MEL-IEL "He who is first in speed"
   5. NO-GAH-EL "He who is first in spirit"
   6. K-ORAB-EIL "He who is first in ecstasy"
   7. L-EV-ANAEL "He who is first in the Secret Wisdom"

IV. Outside the heptagram are the seven names:
   1. ZLLRHIA Zod-el-lar-hee-ah
   2. AZKAAKB Ah-zod-kah-ah-kebeh
   3. PAVPNHR Pah-veh-pen-har
   4. HDMHLAI Heh-dem-hel-ahee
   5. KKAAEEE Keh-kah-ah-eh-eh-eh
   6. IIEELLL Ee-ee-eh-el-le-leh
   7. EELLMG Eh-el-lem-geh

V. Around the outer rim of the seal are two sets of numbers and letters at regular intervals. By an imaginative process of deciphering these curious letters and numbers, the Golden Dawn produced the names of the four elemental Kings (these are not the same as the Kings of the Watchtowers) as follows:
   1. Elemental King of Air. Tahaoelog
   2. Elemental King of Water. Thahebyobeaatanun
   3. Elemental King of Earth. Thahaaothe
   4. Elemental King of Fire. Ohooohaatan

Concerning The Names On The Holy Pantacle.

Although there is no attempt here to describe an invocation ritual for these Angels, the reader may do so if he desires. Using the numerical values contained in Table II for letters, gematria can be used to obtain a specific number for each name. For example, the first name of the second group is "I" which letter can mean either "is" or "is not" and therefore denotes the duality of existence and nonexistence. Its character is solar and its number is 60, the number for the Hebrew word *GAVN* which means "glory" and "sublimity."

The seven great Angels who are each "first" are important deities who preside over the Circles of Heaven (*i.e.* the seven cosmic planes). They should be invoked only with great caution.

THE FOUR GREAT WATCHTOWERS

Dee and Kelly constructed four Tablets, or Watchtowers, one for each of the four quadrants (also called angles) of space. Figure 3 shows an overview of these four great Watchtowers and the Black Cross that unites them together.

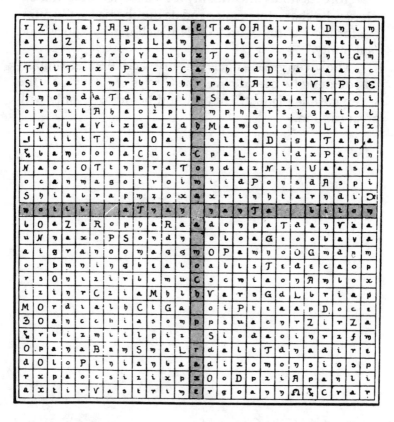

Figure 3. The Four Great Watchtowers Connected by the Black Cross

These Watchtowers are the heart of Enochian Magic just as they represent the heart of the universe. Each

Figure 4 — letter grid:

```
r   Z   i   l   a   f   A^y_u  t   l^i  p   a
a   r   d   Z   a   i   d      p   a    L   a   m
C   z   o   n   s   a   r      o   Y_v  a   u   b
T   o   i   T   t^z_x  o  P     a   c    o   C
S   i   g   a   s   o   n^m    r   b    z   n   h
f   m   o   n   d   a   T      d   i    a   r   l^i
o   r   o   i   b   a   h      a   o    z   p   i
t_c N   a   b   r_a V   i      x   g    a   s_z d
O   i   i   i   t   T   p      a   l    O   a   i
A   b   a   m   o   o   o      a   C^u_v c  a
N   a   o   c   O   T   t      n   p    r   u^a T
o   c   a   n   m   a   g      o   t    r   o   i
S   h   i   a   l   r   a      p   m    z   o   x
```

Figure 4. The First Great Watchtower;
The Great Eastern Quadrant of Air.

Figure 5 — letter grid:

```
T    a    O    A    d    u^v  p    t    D    n    i    m
a^o  a    b^l  c    o    o    r    o    m    e    b    b
T    o^a  g    c    o    n    x^z  m^i  a^nu l    G    m
n    h    o    d    D    i    a    i    l^a  a    o    c
f^p  a    t^c  A    x    i    v^o  V    s    P    x^s  N^Y_h
S    a    a    i    z^x  a    a    r    V    r    L^c  i
m    p    h    a    r    s    l    g    a    i    o    l
M    a    m    g    l    o    i    n    L    i    r    x
o    l    a    a    D    n^a  g    a    T    a    p    a
p    a    L    c    o    i    d    x    P    a    c    n
n    d    a    z    N    z^x  i    V    a    a    s    a
r^i  i    d    P    o    n    s    d    A    s    p    i
x    r    l^r  n    h    t    a    r    n^a  d    i    L
```

Figure 5. The Second Great Watchtower;
The Great Western Quadrant of Water.

b	O	a	Z	a	R	o	p	h	a	R	a
N(u/v)	n	a	x	o	P	S	o	n	d	n	
a	i	g	r	a	n	o	a(o)	m	a	g	g
o	r	p	m	n	i	n	g	b	e	a	l
r	s	O	n	i	z	i	r	l	e	m	u
i	z	i	n	r	C	z	i	a	M	h	l
M	O	r	d	i	a	l	h	C	t	G	a
R(o)	C(O)	a(c)	a(nm)	h(c)	i(h)	(ia/bt)	s(a)	o(s)	m(o)	t(m)	
A	r	b	i	z	m	i	l(1)	l	p	i	z
O	p	a	n	a	l(B)	a	m	S	m	a	T(L)
d	O	l	o	P(F)	l	n	i	a	n	b	a
r	x	p	a	o	c	s	i	z	i	x	p
a	x	t	i	r	V	a	s	t	r	i	m

Figure 6. The Third Great Watchtower;
The Great Northern Quadrant of Earth;

d	o	n	p	a	T	d	a	n	V	a	a
o	l	o	a	G	e	o	o	b	a	u(v)	a(i)
O	P	a	m	n	o	v(o)	G	m(n)	d	n	m
a	P(b)	l	s	T	e	c(d)	e	c	a	o	p
s	c	m	i	o	a	n	A	m	l	o	x
V	a	r	s	G	d	L	b(v)	r	i	a	p
o	i	P	t	e	a	a	p	D	o	c	e
P	s	u(v)	a	c	n	r	Z	i	r	z	a
S	i	o	d	a	o	i	n	r	z	f	m
d	a	l(b)	t	T	d	n	a	d	i	r	e
d	i	x	o	m	o	n	s	i	o	s	p
O	o	D	p	z	i	A	p	a	n	l	i
r	g	o	a	n	n	O(p)	A	C	r	a	r

Figure 7. The Fourth Great Watchtower;
The Great Southern Quadrant of Fire.

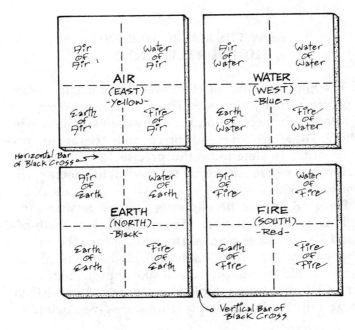

Figure 8. Major subdivisions of the Enochian Tablets.

quadrangle or Tablet is shown separately in Figures 4 through 7 with English equivalents as used by the Golden Dawn. The names of all of the angelic hierarchies of the universe can be found from these Tablets.

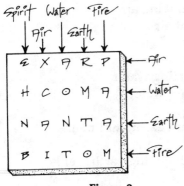

**Figure 9.
The Tablet of Union.**

Surrounding the Watchtowers are thirty concentric circles of increasing radii which represent the thirty Aethyrs, or Aires.

As the Black Cross divides the Tablet into four quadrants, so each quadrant is itself subdivided as shown in Figure 8. The Black Cross is then arranged in the form of a special Tablet called the Tablet of Union as shown in Figure 9.

HOW THE MAGIC WORKS:
THE FOUR ELEMENTS

The Enochian, like all other systems of magic, makes use of four primary elements. These are Earth, Water, Air and Fire and they correspond to many things, as shown in Table IV. These attributes and correspondences are important in order to determine the precise location on the Watchtowers where one wishes to travel, or to select a spirit to converse with.

Figure 8 shows the elements as they relate to the Watchtowers. Combinations of elements such as Earth-of-Air and Fire-of-Water are made to better specify the nature of the locality. A visit to Water-of-Earth in the north for example, could be interpreted as a lake or pond. Similarly, Earth-of-Water in the west could be interpreted as an island or large ship. Additional explanations are given below.

1. Fire of Fire, Aries, Violent fire
2. Air of Fire, Leo, continuous fire
3. Water of Fire, Sagittarius, reflective fire
4. Earth of Fire, dispersiveness
5. Fire of Air, Libra, violent wind
6. Air of Air, Aquarius, steady moving air
7. Water of Air, Gemini, stagnant air
8. Earth of Air, flexibility
9. Fire of Water, Cancer, violent water
10. Air of Water, Scorpio, evaporating water
11. Water of Water, Pisces, stagnant water
12. Earth of Water, cohesiveness
13. Fire of Earth, Capricorn, violent earth, mountains
14. Air of Earth, Taurus, Flat earth, plains
15. Water of Earth, Virgo, quiet life-giving earth, fields
16. Earth of Earth, solidity

TABLE IV. CORRESPONDENCE WITH
THE FOUR ELEMENTS

	Earth	Water	Air	Fire
Symbol	▽	▽	△	△
Plane	Physical	Astral	Mental	Spiritual
Property	Cold	Cold	Hot	Hot
	Dry	Moist	Moist	Dry
Residents	Gnomes	Undines	Sylphs	Salamanders
Astrological	Taurus	Cancer	Gemini	Aries
Signs	Virgo	Scorpio	Libra	Leo
	Capricorn	Pisces	Aquarius	Sagittarius
Planets	Venus	Mars	Saturn	Sun
	Moon		Mercury	Jupiter
Tarot	Pantacles	Cups	Swords	Wands
Quadrant	Northern	Western	Eastern	Southern
Color	Black	Blue	Yellow	Red

HOW THE MAGIC WORKS: THE FIFTH ELEMENT

In addition to the four elements of the Watchtowers, a fifth element, Spirit, is used in Enochian Magic. This element is assigned to the Tablet of Union. The symbol for Spirit is a spoked wheel ✹ and its color is white. Together, these five elements are symbolized by the five-pointed pentagram (Figure 16). Usually the element Spirit is assigned to the topmost point. When the pentagram is inverted, the four elements are over Spirit (and therefore have supremacy). This is said to be an unholy sign, used only in operations of black magic. The reason for this is that Spirit has a natural supremacy over the four elements of Earth, Water, Air and Fire (they are, in fact, expressions of Spirit) and any reversal is therefore unnatural.

GREAT SECRET HOLY NAMES

The four quadrants each give a great secret Holy Name of God along its middle row (called the "Linea Spiritus Sancti"). Each name is three words having 3, 4, and 5 letters:

1. **Air.** The Air quadrant contains the name
   ORO-IBAH-AOZPI (OROI-BAHAO-Z-PI)
   This name is pronounced *Oh-roh-Ee-bah-Ah-oh-zod-pee* and means
   "He who cries aloud in the place of desolation."

2. **Water.** The Water quadrant contains the name
   MPH-ARSL-GAIOL (MPH-ARS-L-G-IA-OL)
   This name is pronounced *Em-Peh-heh-Ar-ess-el-Gah-ee-oh-leh* and means
   "He who is the first true creator; the horned one."

3. **Earth.** The Earth quadrant contains the name
   MOR-DIAL-HKTGA (MORD-IAL-HKT-GA)
   This name is pronounced *Moh-ar-Dee-ah-leh-Heh-keh-teh-gah* and means
   "He who burns up iniquity without equal."

4. **Fire.** The Fire quadrant contains the name
   OIP-TEAA-PDOKE (OI-P-TEA-AP-DO-KE)
   This name is pronounced *Oh-ee-peh-Teh-ah-ah-Peh-doh-keh* and means
   "He whose name is unchanged from what it was."

Correct Pronouncement of the Holy Names.

The four great secret Holy Names should be pronounced in one long flowing breath. However, emphasis should be given to the first syllable of each name section. For example, ORO-IBAH-AOZPI should be spoken with emphasis on the Oh, Ee, and Ah syllables which begin each section of the name.

An alternate method of pronunciation is to pause briefly after each section. This results in saying three distinct names. For example, one could say *Oh-roh Ee-bah Ah-oh-zod-pee.* Either method is effective. The student should experiment with both and then choose the way that works best for him.

Gematria of the Four Great Holy Names.

1. **ORO-IBAH-AOZPI** is 340, the number for the Enochian word ZOKH meaning "the past," and the Hebrew word PRS meaning "Vulture" (the vulture was used by the ancient Egyptians to symbolize motherhood).

2. **MPH-ARSL-GAIOL** is 333, the number for the Enochian phrase SIAION-GRAA which means "temple of the moon." It is also the number for the Hebrew spelling of ChURUNZUN (I.E. Choronzon), the Demon of the tenth Aethyr and is half of 666, the number of the Beast of the Apocalypse which Crowley assumed for himself. The serious student should not be at all intimidated by this. The number 666 is equal to the Hebrew word IThRUN which means "good."

3. **MOR-DIAL-HKTGA** is 622, the number for the Enochian phrase PIAP-PATRALX which means "balance of stone," and the Hebrew word RKTh meaning "blessings."

4. **OIP-TEAA-PDOKE** is 483, the number for the Enochian phrase LRING-MONONS which means "to stir up the heart," and the Hebrew phrase GRM SPQ which means "to cause doubt."

5. The gematria of the Hebrew words used above are calculated using standard Hebrew gematric values (reference Crowley's *LIBER 777*) as follows:

PRS = 80+200+60 = 340

ChURUNZUN = 8+6+200+6+50+7+6+50 = 333

IThRUN = 10+400+200+6+50 = 666
BRKTh = 2+200+20+400 = 622
GRM SPQ = 3+200+40+60+80+100 = 483

General Meaning and Use of the Four Great Holy Names

The four great secret Holy Names are not usually invoked by themselves, being but names of God. Normally, the names are used in ritual invocations of the Kings, Seniors, Archangels, or Angels of the entire Watchtowers, to get an initial feel or mood of the particular Watchtower under consideration. Each name reflects the general atmosphere of its respective quadrant and should be used with great care. The meaning of the name must be clearly held in mind when the name is spoken.

1. **ORO-IBAH-AOZPI.** This colors the Watchtower of Air with an atmosphere of great age and of endless past events. The formless aspect of air gives the feeling of emptiness and desolation.

2. **MPH-ARSL-GAIOL.** This colors the Watchtower of Water with an atmosphere of creation and birth. The life-giving aspect of water gives the feeling of form coming out of formlessness.

3. **MOR-DIAL-HKTGA.** This colors the Watchtower of Earth with an atmosphere of stability and equalibrium. The solidifying aspect of earth gives the feeling of opposing forces becoming balanced, of chaos becoming structured.

4. **OIP-TEAA-PDOKE.** This colors the Watchtower of Fire with an atmosphere of instability and turmoil. The violent aspect of fire gives the feeling of continuous dissociation.

THE FOUR GREAT KINGS

How to Obtain Their Names.

Each quadrant has a presiding King or ruler. The name of each Great King is obtained from the center of each respective Tablet by making a clockwise circle, as shown in Figure 10 below for water.

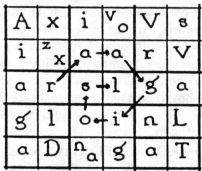

Figure 10. The Name of the King of Water from the Center of the Second Watchtower

The Names of the Four Great Kings.

Air: The name of the King of Air is BATAIVAH (BA-TA-I-VAH). This is pronounced *Bah-tah-ee-vah-heh* and means "He whose voice seems to have wings."

Water: The name of the King of Water is RAAGIOSL (RAA-GI-OSL). This is pronounced *Rah-ah-gee-oh-sel* and means "He whose hands are toward the East."

Earth: The name of the King of Earth is IKZH$^I_N$$^H_K$AL (I-KZH-I-KAL). This is pronounced *Ee-keh-zod-hee-kal* and means "He who solidifies the past."

Fire: The name of the King of Fire is EDLPRNAA (ED-L-PRNAA). This is pronounced *Eh-del-par-nah-ah* and means "He who is first to receive the flames."

General Character and Qualities of the Four Great Kings

Using gematria on the names of the four Great Kings will give hints of their true nature, as shown in Table V. These Kings can be either invoked or visited by the magician. While speaking the name, the character and qualities of the King must be firmly held in mind. These are:

The King of Air, BATAIVAH, is kindly and loving. His nature is feminine. He bestows mercy and grace and he speaks with a beautiful voice. In fact his words seem like heavenly music, which is both pleasant and seductive.

The King of Water, RAAGIOSL, is creative and is always making things. His nature, being reflective, is such that one often sees one's own worst faults manifested in him. He seeks, through life-giving creativity, to reduce infinite spiritual ideas into finite forms.

The King of Earth, IKZHIKAL, lives in the past. He hates change. He strives to keep things as they are. He loves to describe and define things. He gave all things of the earth their original names, and he seeks to keep them bound to these names.

The King of Fire, EDLPRNAA, is a consuming fiery being, dangerous and easy to provoke to anger. He loves change and hates stagnation. He has a violent temper and seeks to disperse all aggregates into their monadic essence. The inexperienced magician would do well to avoid this King until he is adept at invocations.

TABLE V.
GEMATRIA OF THE FOUR GREAT KINGS

NAME	NUMERICAL VALUE	KEY EQUIVALENT WORD ENOCHIAN	HEBREW
King of Air, BATAIVAH	163	RIT (mercy)	NVQBH (a woman)
also	157	SORGE (love)	NQBH (female)
King of Water, RAAGIOSL	225	MOOOAH-OL (the happiness of making things)	HChZRH (reflection)
King of Earth, IKZHIKAL	744	KAL-HOLQ-KAOSG (to solidify and measure) also 744 = 31 x 24: where 31 = BESZ (matter) 24 = TAFA (poison)	
King of Fire, (Alternate:	193	BAEOUIBS (the righteous one)	
EDLPRNAAH	194	BITOM (fire)	TzDQ (justice)

THE TWENTY-FOUR SENIORS

How To Obtain Their Names.

The Tablets contain the names of 24 Seniors or Elders; six in each quadrant. These are found in the center row and two center columns of each quadrant by reading from the center outward (or upward and downward). Each name contains seven letters, except when double letters are given in a section. Figure 11 shows the derivation of the Seniors from the Watchtower of Air as an example.

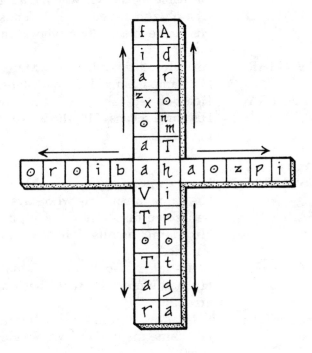

**Figure 11. The Derivation of the Six Seniors
from the Great Watchtower of Air.**

The Names of the Twenty-Four Seniors.

Name	Pronunciation	Planetary Correspondence
I. Air		
1. HABIORO	Hah-bee-oh-roh	Mars
	His name means "He whose voice is low."	
2. AAO^Z_XAIF	Ah-ah-oh-zodah-ee-feh	Jupiter
	His name means "He who frequents the ways."	
3. HT^N_MORDA	Heh-teh-noh-rah-dah	Luna
	His name means "He who has a son."	
4. AHAOZAPI	Aha-oh-zodah-pee	Venus
	His name means "He who is in his place."	
5. AVTOTAR	Ah-veh-toh-tah-rah	Mercury
	His name means "He who listens."	
6. HIPOTGA	Hee-poh-teh-gah	Saturn
	His name means "He who is like nothing else."	
II. Water		
1. LSRAHPM	Less-rah-pem	Mars
	His name means "He who slays."	
2. SAIINO^U_V	Sah-ee-ee-noh-veh	Jupiter
	His name means "He who has a temple."	
3. LA^V_OA^X_ZRP	El-ah-vahtz-ar-peh	Luna
	His name means "He who is first in arrogance."	
4. SLGAIOL	Sel-gah-ee-oh-leh	Venus
	His name means "He who made the spirit."	
5. SO^N_AI^Z_XNT	Soh-ahee-zoden-teh	Mercury
	His name means "He who has the saving waters."	

6. LIGDISA   Elee-geh-dee-sah   Saturn
His name means "He who has no head."

III. Earth
1. LAIDROM   El-ahee-dar-oh-em   Mars
His name means "He who knows the secrets of truth."
2. AKZINOR   Ah-keh-zodee-noh-rah   Jupiter
His name means "He who is from the dark waters."
3. LZINOPO   El-zodee-noh-poh   Luna
His name means "He who is first in the deep waters."
4. ALHKTGA   Ah-leh-hek-teh-gah   Venus
His name means "He who is most like a spirit."
5. $A^H_K M^L_B LKV$ Ah-mel-el-keh-veh   Mercury
His name means "He who is most ancient."
6. $L^L_H IANSA$ Elee-ee-ah-ness-ah   Saturn
His name means "He who is first in truth."

IV. Fire.
1. AAETPIO   Ah-ah-eteh-pee-oh   Mars
His name means "He who seeks his place."
2. ADAEOET   Ah-dah-eh-oh-eteh   Jupiter
His name means "He who sings like a bird."
3. $ALN^K_D{}^V_O OD$ Ah-len-keh-voh-deh   Luna
His name means "He who will serve herein."
4. AAPDOKE   Ah-ah-ped-oh-keh   Venus
His name means "He whose name remains the same."

5. ANODOIN   Ah-noh-doh-ee-neh   Mercury

His name means "He who is open to others."

6. ARINNA^OP   Ah-ree-neh-nah-peh   Saturn

His name means "He who protects with a sword."

Gematria of the Twenty-Four Seniors.

Each Senior has a numerical value obtained by summing up the appropriate letter values as contained in Table II. Using gematria, the name of each Senior corresponds to key Enochian words or phrases which have a direct bearing on their natures. An example of selected numerical correspondences is in Table VI.

TABLE VI. GEMATRIA OF THE NAMES OF THE SENIORS

Name	Numerical Value	Key Corresponding Word or Phrase
Air:		
HABIORO	232	VRANA (an elder)
AAOZAIF	120	graa (moon), OM (knowledge)
	114	BABALOND (seductress)
HTNORDA	200	LIALPRT (First Flame)
	194	BITOM (fire), PARADIZ (virgin)
AHAOZPI	121	HOM (to live), NANTA (earth)
	115	EOLIS (to make), HARG (to plant)
AVTOTAR	230	ROR (the sun)
HIPOTGA	123	MOZ (joy)
Water:		
LSRAHPM	221	MALPRG (fiery flames)
SAIINOV	283	PIRIPSOL (heaven)
LAVAXRP	599	OXI-DOSIG (mighty dark one)
SLGAIOL	127	PRGE (fire), IADNAH (knowledge)
SOAIZNT	171	APOPHRASZ (motion)
	165	SOE-GONO (faithful savior)
	159	NOQOLH (servant)
LIGDISA	153	SA-F-ORS (one in darkness)
Earth:		
LAIDROM	298	ZORGE-BRGDO (restful sleep)
AKZINOR	555	PAPNOR-KAOSG (memory of earth)
	549	TA-L-PATRALX (lie the first stone)
LZINOPO	196	TABAAN-GRAA (ruler of the moon)
	190	QUASAHI (bliss)
AHMLLKV	483[a]	TABAAN-KHIDAO (ruler of diamonds)
ALHKTGA	338	DODRMNI (vexed)
LIIANSA	197	QUASAHIS (one who delights)
Fire:		
AAETPIO	130	SOBOLN (west), VNPH (anger)
	124	GNAY (action)
ADAEOET	75	NAZPS (a sword)
	69	ZEN (sacrifice)
ALNKVOD	468	BALZARG-YARRY (steward of fate)
AAPDOKE	365	TABAAM-PIRIPSOL (ruler of the heavens)
ANODOIN	230	ROR (the sun) Note: see AVTOTAR of Air.
ARINNAP	281	MALPIRG (fires of life)

[a]483 is also OIP-TEAA-PDOKE, the Holy Name of the Watchtower of Fire.

HOW THE MAGIC WORKS: THE PLANETS

The seven sacred planets represent seven planetary spheres, or zones of influence. The fact that two of these planets are the Sun and the Moon, which are not really "planets" as such, does not alter the fact of their respective influences. The most important correspondences are:

Planet	Sign	Chief Characteristics	Watchtower Subquadrant Influenced
Saturn	♄	Intuition,thought formation	Earth of Air
Jupiter	♃	Harmony, beneficial change	Water of Fire
Mars	♂	Destruction, conflicting manifestation	Earth of Fire
Sun	☉	Creativity, active change	Air of Fire
Venus	♀	Emotions, instincts	Water of Earth
Mercury	☿	Intellect, reflective thought	Water of Air
Moon	☽	Reflection, passive manifestation, formation of emotions	Earth of Water

HOW TO INVOKE THE KINGS AND SENIORS

The cross shown in Figure 11 is called the Great Cross of the Watchtower. The Holy Names, and the names of the Kings and Seniors, are all taken from the Great Cross. Any one of the Kings and Seniors can be invoked by using the Hexagram Ritual (see below). Each King is attributed to the Sun. Each Senior is attributed to a planet, as shown earlier. A hexagram has six points and each corresponds to a planet, and therefore to a Senior. During the ritual, a hexagram is drawn for a particular Senior by beginning it at the appropriate point. The hexagram is shown in Figure 12. In order to invoke a King, it can be seen that there is no point on the hexagram for the Sun. A King is invoked by drawing all six planetary hexagrams as shown in Figure 13.

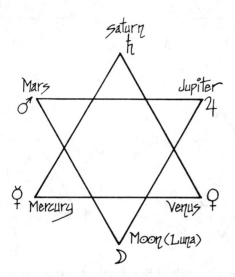

Figure 12. Hexagram for Invocation and Banishment of Kings and Seniors.

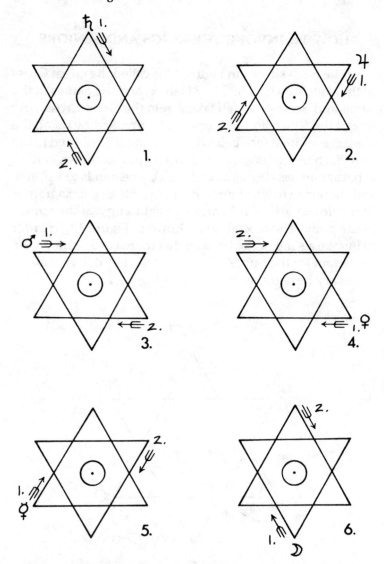

Figure 13. The Six Invoking Hexagrams for Kings. For each hexagram begin at the point shown and in the direction of the arrow as indicated. Do triangle 1 first, then triangle 2.

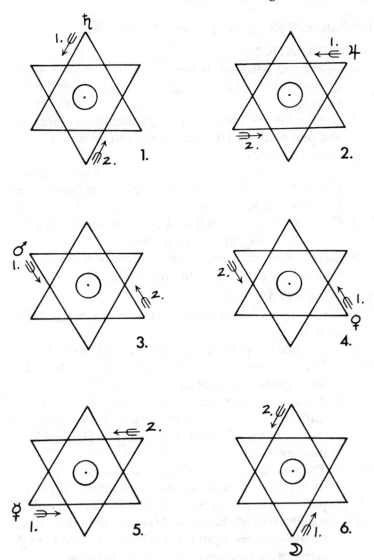

Figure 14. The Six Banishing Hexagrams for Kings. For each hexagram begin at the point shown and in the direction of the arrow as indicated. Do triangle 1 first, then triangle 2.

Invocation of Kings and Seniors: Step By Step.

A. PREPARATION

1. Select the King or Senior to be invoked. This will depend upon the motive or purpose for the invocation.
2. Determine the corresponding Watchtower, element, and planetary sign (if a King is chosen, all six planetary signs are used).
3. Memorize the pronunciation of all names involved (Holy Name, King and, if invoking a Senior, the Senior's name).
4. Consult Figures 12, 13, and 14 to determine the appropriate hexagrams to be drawn.
5. Stand facing the appropriate Watchtower (*i.e.* North, South, East or West, from Figure 8).

B. INVOCATION

1. Trace a hexagram in the air with either a magic Wand or Rod.
   a. Begin at the point of the hexagram shown in Figure 12 that corresponds to the Senior's planet. If a King, then always begin at Saturn (top).
   b. Trace a line from that point and continue clockwise until a triangle has been drawn. This is the first triangle (no. 1 in each hexagram of Figure 13) of the hexagram.
   c. The starting point of the second triangle (no. 2 in each of the hexagrams shown in Figure 13) is the point opposite the Senior's planet. For example, if the first triangle began on Mercury, then the second would start on Jupiter. For a King, the first triangle starts on Saturn and the second on Luna.
   d. Trace a line from that point and continue clockwise until a triangle is drawn. This is the second triangle and completes the hexagram.

e. Imagination is important here. As the magician traces each line, he imagines that a line is actually being drawn in the air before him. The color of this psychic construction is as follows:

If the starting point is:	The the color of the hexagram is:
Saturn	deep red or crimson
Jupiter	deep violet
Mars	orange
Venus	amber
Mercury	violet-purple
Luna	deep violet-blue or indigo

f. To further tax the imagination, after any hexagram is drawn, imagine the planetary symbol (as given in Figure 12) at the center of the hexagram. Figure 13 shows the Sun sign inside each of the hexagrams drawn for a King.

g. A Senior needs only one hexagram to be invoked. However, a King must have all six. for each of the four Great Kings, begin with a Saturn hexagram, then draw one for Jupiter, then Mars, then Venus, then Mercury and lastly for Luna (for certain occult reasons, this order is very important here).

2. With the complete hexagram(s) imagined in shining color, repeat the corresponding secret Holy Name and then the King's name (and then the Senior's name if a Senior is being invoked). Concentrate on the known character traits of these names. If successful, he will appear in the hexagram in some form and converse with the magician. If partially successful, the magician may catch an idea or thought from him.

3. *Success or failure is not measured by requiring that a King or Senior physically jump out at the magician. It is measured*

only by the degree in achievement of the original motive. Success or failure may come days or even months after the operation.

C. BANISHMENT

1. Every spirit invoked, must be banished after the operation. If unsure whether the invocation was successful or not, use the banishment ritual anyway (just in case).
2. To banish a King or Senior back to his region, simply go through the hexagrams again, but this time begin counterclockwise rather than clockwise. This has the effect of reversing the invocation. (An example of how to banish a King is in Figure 14.)

HOW THE MAGIC WORKS: INCENSE

Although the use of incense during a magical operation is optional, an appropriate incense sometimes helps to assist the mind to concentrate. It also helps stimulate the imagination, which can be critical to success. The following list shows the corresponding incense for each subquadrant and can be used for both invocations and traveling in the Spirit Vision:

⊕ of ⊕ Ambergris.

△ of ⊕ The Gall of Rukh.

▽ of ⊕ Onycha.

▽̶ of ⊕ Musk.

△̶ of ⊕ Civet.

⊕ of △ Lign-aloes.

△ of △ Galbanum.

▽ of △ Mastick.

▽̶ of △ Storax.

△̶ of △ Olibanum.

⊕ of ▽ Myrrh.

△ of ▽ Camphor.

▽ of ▽ Siamese Benzoin.

▽̶ of ▽ Indigo.

△̶ of ▽ Opoponax.

⊕ of ▽̶ Dittany of Crete.

△ of ▽̶ Assafoetida.

▽ of ▽̶ Clover.

▽̶ of ▽̶ Storax.

△̶ of ▽̶ Benzoin.

⊕ of △̶ Saffron.

△ of △̶ Lign-aloes.

▽ of △̶ Red-sanders.

▽̶ of △̶ Red Sandalwood.

△̶ of △̶ Olibanum.

The following list gives the type of incense to be used for corresponding planetary influences:

Saturn	myrrh, sulphur, indigo (*exercise caution with sulphur*)
Jupiter	Cedar, saffron
Mars	tobacco, pepper
Sun	olibanum, cinnamon
Venus	rose, benzoin, sandalwood, myrtle
Mercury	storax, mace, mastic
Moon	jasmine, ginseng, camphor, aloes

The following list gives the type of incense to be used to correspond with the elements:

Air	galbanum, peppermint, any light uplifting odor
Water	myrrh, onycha, any purgative odor
Earth	storax, any dull heavy odor
Fire	olibanum, any fiery odor

If the incenses listed above are unavailable, the following can be substituted:

Saturn	any odorous roots such as pepperwort
Jupiter	any odorous fruits such as coconut
Mars	any odorous woods such as pine or cedar
Sun	any odorous gums such as musk or anise
Venus	any odorous flowers such as roses or violets
Mercury	any odorous seeds such as bay berries
Moon	any odorous vegetable leaves such as myrtle or bay
Earth	any dry, heavy, earthy scent such as musk or sandalwood
Water	any cool, watery scent such as ginger
Air	any light, airy scent such as lemon or orange
Fire	any spicy or fiery scent such as cinnamon

Possible sources for incense are:

Auroma International,
   P.O. Box 2, Wilmot, WI 53192
Spencer Gifts, Inc.,
   Atlantic City NJ 08411
Nature Scents, Olfactory,
   West Los Angeles, CA 90064
The Magickal Childe,
   35 West 19 Street, New York, NY 10011
International Imports,
   P.O. Box 2010, Toluca Lake, CA 91602

INVOCATION OF A SENIOR

Suppose, for an example, one would like to improve one's appreciation for music. Such a boon could be granted by the Senior, ADAEOET, "He who sings like a bird." The magician begins by facing South toward the great Watchtower of Fire, where ADAEOET dwells.

He wears only a robe, or at least very loose-fitting and comfortable clothing. The real importance of clothing is that it must be of a type that can be forgotten or ignored. Tight clothing can interfere with concentration, and for that reason should not be worn. The same can be said for nudity; it is good if one can forget the body and not good if one feels at all awkward or uncomfortable. The magician must be able to forget his body for a while. Anything that aids this is good while, on the other hand, anything that hinders this is bad.

All distracting thoughts and concerns must be cast aside. Total concentration is mandatory.

The magician raises his arms outward toward the South and calls out the Holy Name,

"OIP-TEAA-PDOKE, may my request be granted. You who are unchanged by time, hear me.

OIP-TEAA-PDOKE, thou most holy name. You are the Watchtower of the South. You are the Watchtower of Fire. All things return to you. Hear me.

LRING-MONONS, I call upon you for your music, OIP-TEAA-PDOKE."

The magician then calls upon the King of Fire:

"EDLPRNAA, O Receiver of the Flames, thou who art King over Fire, assist me. Make me to be a knower of music.

EDLPRNAAH, BITOM, EDLPRNAAH, change me, renew me in your forge.

BITOM, I desire to be changed. I desire to be made

55

anew. EDLPRNAAH, BITOM, EDLPRNAAH."

The magician now feels the presence of the King of Fire near him. He should feel the violent churning of this fiery quadrant around him. Now he takes his Fire Wand (preferably one he has made himself) and traces a large hexagram in the air before him. This hexagram is deep violet and is drawn as shown in hexagram no. 2 of Figure 13 (*i.e.* the Jupiter Hexagram). He sees a violet "♃" glistening in the center, which charges the hexagram with a tone both religious and creative (if incense is used to heighten the proper mood here, it should be of cedar or saffron).

As the magician gazes into the sparkling violet hexagram of Jupiter, he makes the final invocation:

"ADAEOET, whose voice is music, allow me to share your songs, O ADAEOET.

May your sword cut away my ignorance. May I become new. May my old self be sacrificed as it is in ZEN, the eighteenth Aethyr. May I rise up new with your attributes. May I share your music, O ADAEOET, GOHO, ZEN, TOL-BALT, ADAEOET."

Now the magician feels himself changing under the influence of fire and music. He imagines ADAEOET in the hexagram showering forth his musical ability. He sees himself as a new person. He is now one who loves and appreciates music. His own inherent abilities will now surely be enhanced.

In gratitude to ADAEOET, he now banishes the Senior with a banishing hexagram (hexagram no. 2 in Figure 14). ADAEOET thus returns to the Watchtower of Fire in the South.

No Senior, or any other spirit for that matter, can make something from nothing. They can only work within specific occult laws. Here the magician does not ask for the impossible. He already has a musical ability (as everyone does) buried in his subconscious. He asks only that it be brought out into manifestation. This ADAEOET can do. If properly carried out, this invocation will be effective in some degree. Although the magician will probably not be able to sit immediately at a piano and play Handel or Bach, he probably will find that taking piano lessons is surprisingly easy and that, with practice, he can play tolerably well.

INVOCATION *vs* SPIRIT VISION

The correspondences between the four elements and the four directions of space, as given for invocations, are:

1. The East Winds are airy therefore Air is in the East.
2. The South winds are hot and dry therefore Fire is in the South.
3. The West Winds are moist with rain therefore Water is in the West.
4. The North Winds are cold and dry therefore Earth is in the North.

These correspondences are in accord with the winds, and in accord with ancient Egyptian tradition. However, whenever astral traveling or moving in the "Spirit Vision" is used, the traditional Zodiac correspondences may be used. These are:

1. Air in the West
2. Water in the North
3. Earth in the South
4. Fire in the East

As a general rule: to invoke, stand facing the position of the winds because the Earth is subject to the winds. However, to travel in the Spirit Vision, face the positions according to the Zodiac.

THE ANGELS OF THE CALVARY CROSS

Each Lesser Angel (*i.e.* each subquadrant or angle, such as Water of Air) has a cross called the "Sephirothic Calvary Cross". Figure 15 shows the four Calvary Crosses of the Watchtower of Earth as an example. There is a total of sixteen Calvary crosses. Each cross contains ten squares corresponding to the ten Sephiroth of the Hebrew Qabalah.

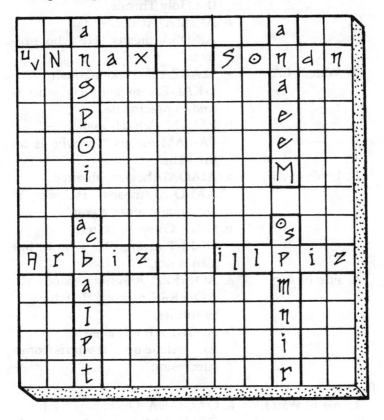

Figure 15. Four Calvary Crosses in the Great Watchtower of Earth.

Each Calvary Cross contains two names. Reading downward is a six-lettered name and across is a five-lettered name. The former name evokes the intelligent forces of that subquadrant, while the latter name control them. These Calvary Cross Names are:

I. Air

    1. Air of Air: a. IDOIGO Ee-doh-ee-goh IDOIGO means "He who sits on the Holy Throne."

                                b. ARDZA Ar-deh-zodah AR-DSA means "He who protects."

    2. Water of Air: a. $_h$LAKZAEl-lah-keh-zodah L-KAL-ZA means "He who is first to precipitate."

                                b. PALAM Pah-lah-meh PA-LAM means "He who is on the Path."

    3. Earth of Air: a. AIAOAIAhee-ah-oh-ahee AAI-O-AI means "He who is within and among you."

                                b. OIIIT Ohee-ee-ee-teh OI-I-I-T means "He who is, but also is not."

    4. Fire of Air: a. AO-^{Uv}RRZ Ah-oh-var-razod AO-VRRS means "He who beautifies."

                                b. ALOAI Ah-loh-ahee ALO-AI means "He who is from a succession."

II. Water

    1. Air of Water: a. O-^{B}$_L$GO-^{T}$_K$A Oh-beh-goh-tah OBLOG-TA means "He who is like a garland."

b. $^A_OA^B_LKO$ Ah-ah-beh-koh
ABA-KO means "He who is bent over."

1. Water of Water: a. NELAPR En-el-ah-par
N-ELAP-R means "He who must have his way."

b. OMEBB Oh-meb-beh
OM-EBB means "He who knows."

3. Earth of Water: a. MALAD-^{I}R Em-ah-lah-dee
MAL-ADI means "He who shoots arrows."

b. OLAAD Oh-lah-ah-deh
OL-ADA means "He who created birds."

4. Fire of Water: a. IAAASD Ee-ah-ah-ah-ess-deh
IA-A-ASD means "He who is in truth."

b. ATAPA Ah-tah-pah
A-TA-PA means "He who bears a likeness."

III. Earth

1. Air of Earth: a. ANGPOI Ah-neh-geh-pohee
ANG-POI means "He who divides thoughts."

b. ^{U}vNNAX Ven-nahtz
VN-N-AX means "He whose great name is All."

2. Water of Earth: a. ANAEEM Ah-nah-eh-eh-meh
ANA-E-EM means "He who is nine times obedient."

b. SONDN Soh-neh-den
S-ONDN means "He who has a kingdom."

3. Earth of Earth: a. ^{A}кBALPT Ah-bah-leh-peh-teh
ABA-LPT means "He who stoops down."

b. ARBIZ Ar-bee-zod
AR-BI-Z means "He whose voice protects."

4. Fire of Earth: a. ^OsPMNIR Oh-pem-nee-ar
OM-PNIR means "He who increases knowledge."

b. ¹ʟLPIZ Eel-pee-zod
IL-PI-Z means "He whose place is the Aethyrs."

IV. Fire.
1. Air of Fire: a. NOALMR Noh-ah-leh-mar
NOA-L-MR means "He who is first to bring about torment."

b. OLOAG Oh-loh-ah-geh
OL-OAG means "He who makes nothing."

2. Water of Fire: a. VADALI Vah-dah-lee
V-LAIAD means "He who has the Secret Truth."

b. OBA^{Uv}A₁ Oh-bah-vah
OBA-V-IA means "He who has half of truth."

3. Earth of Fire: a. ^UvO-¹ʙXDO Voh-letz-doh
VOLX-DO means "He whose name is Annihilation."

b. SIODA Ess-ee-oh-dah
S-IO-DA means "He who is eternal."

4. Fire of Fire: a. RZIONR Rah-zodee-oh-nar
ZIN-ROR means "He who is in the Waters of the Sun."

b. NRZFM En-rah-zod-eff-em
NRZ-F-M means "He who visits here six times."

THE KERUBIC ANGELS OR KERUBIM

Above the horizontal bar of each Calvary Cross are four letters, two on each side of the vertical bar. These four letters form the name of a Kerubic Angel, one for each subquadrant. Each of these names can be anagramed, or anagramatized transposed, to form three other names. Together this totals 64 Kerubic Angels: 16 in each Watchtower and four in each subquadrant.

I. Air.
1. Air of Air: RZLA (Ra-zodel-ah), ZLAR, LARZ, ARZL
2. Water of Air: ^Y_UTPA (Yuh-teh-pah), TPA^Y_U, PA^Y_UT, A^Y_UYP
3. Earth of Air: ^T_KNB^R_A (Ten-beh-rah), NB$^T_K{}^R_A$, B$^T_K{}^R_A$N, $^T_K{}^R_A$NB
4. Fire of Air: XG^S_ZD (Tz-egg-seh-deh), G^S_ZDX, ^S_ZDXG, DXG^S_Z

II. Water.
1. Air of Water: TAAD (Tah-ah-deh), AADT, ADTA, DTAA
2. Water of Water: TDIM (Teh-dee-em), DIMI, IMTD, MTDI
3. Earth of Water: MAGL (Em-ah-gel), AGLM, GLMA, LMAG
4. Fire of Water: NLRX (En-el-artz), LRXN, RXNL, XNLR

III. Earth.
1. Air of Earth: BOZA (Boh-zodah), OZAB, ZABO, ABOZ
2. Water of Earth: PHRA (Peh-har-ah), HRAP, RAPH, APHR

3. Earth of Earth: $^R_oK_oN_AK_{NM}$ (Roh-koh-nah-kem),
   $^K_oN_AK_{NM}{}^R$, $^N_AK_{NM}{}^R_oK_o$,
   $^K_{NM}{}^R_oK_oN_A$

4. Fire of Earth: $^{IA}_{BT}{}^.S_AM_oT_M$ (Ee-ah-sah-moh-tem),
   $^S_AM_oT_{M\text{-}BT}{}^{.IA}{}^-$, $^M_oT_{M\text{-}BT}{}^{.IA}{}^-S_A$,
   $^T_{M\text{-}BT}{}^{.IA}S_AM_o$

IV. Fire.

1. Air of Fire: DOPA (Doh-pah), OPAD, PADO, ADOP

2. Water of Fire: ANAA (An-ah-ah), NAAA, AAAN, AANA

3. Earth of Fire: PSAK (Pess-ah-keh), SAKP, AKPS, KPSA

4. Fire of Fire: ZIZA (Zodee-zodah), IZAZ, ZAZI, AZIZ*

What the Kerubim Govern

Each of the Kerubic Angels governs that file of squares which begins with its first letter. For example, in the Watchtower of Air, the Kerubic Angel RZLA governs that area of the subquadrant Air of Air that contains the letters R(A)KTSF. In the same way, ZLAR rules over the file of Z(R)ZOIM, LARZ rules over L(Z)NTAN and ARZL rules over A(A)STSD. In each case, the second letter is placed in parenthesis to show that it is a part of the Calvary Cross. It is not governed by the Kerubic Angel but by the Calvary Cross Angel.

---

*According to the Golden Dawn, AZIZ is a huge human-shaped being, fiery red with flaming wings and emerald green hair.
ZAZI is black and white, flaming and flashing.
IZAZ is blue and orange and covered with a fiery mist.
ZIZA is orange with hazy gold wings which are like gauze, and he has nets of gold around him.

THE ARCHANGELS

In addition to the 64 Kerubim, there are also 64 Archangels who rule over them. The names of these Archangels are found by prefixing one letter from the Tablet of Union or Black Cross to the names of the Kerubim. The letters used are E, H, N and B. These are the first letters of each row as shown in Figure 9 and refer to the element Spirit.

1. "E" prefixes the Kerubic Angels of Air:
   Air. ERZLA Er-zodel-ah
   Water. E$^{Y}_{U}$TPA Eh-yuh-teh-pah
   Earth. E$^{T}_{K}$NB$^{R}_{A}$ Eh-ten-beh-rah
   Fire. EXG$^{S}_{Z}$D Ehtz-egg-seh-deh
   Similarly for the 12 lesser Kerubic Angels of Air.

2. "H" prefixes the Kerubic Angels of Water.
   Air. HTAAD Heh-tah-ah-deh
   Water. HTDIM Heh-teh-dee-em
   Earth. HMAGL Hem-ah-gel
   Fire. HNLRX Hen-el-artz
   Similarly for the 12 lesser Kerubic Angels of Water.

3. "N" prefixes the Kerubic Angels of Earth.
   Air. NBOZA En-boh-zodah
   Water. NPHRA Enpeh-har-ah
   Earth. N$^{R}_{O}$K$_{O}$N$_{A}$K$_{NM}$ En-roh-koh-nah-kem
   Fire. N-$^{IAS}_{BT}$A$^{T}_{O}$M Enee-ah-sah-moh-tem
   Similarly for the 12 lesser Kerubic Angels of Earth.

4. "B" prefixes the Kerubic Angels of Fire.
   Air. BDOPA Beh-doh-pah
   Water. BANAA Ban-ah-ah
   Earth. BPSAK Beh-pess-ah-keh
   Fire. BZIZA Beh-zodee-zodah
   Similarly for the 12 lesser Kerubic Angels of Fire.

Chief Characteristics of the Archangels and Kerubim

The Archangels and Kerubim of the sixteen subquadrants, are characterized according to their locality as follows:

1. *Archangels and Kerubim of the four Air subquadrants.* These Angels are characterized by pairs of opposing forces such as expansion and contraction, attraction and repulsion, solidification and dispersion. They seek a balance between such dual forces.

2. *Archangels and Kerubim of the four Water subquadrants.* These Angels are characterized by motion. They desire continual movement and flux. They seek change in all things.

3. *Archangels and Kerubim of the four Earth subquadrants.* These Angels are characterized by their desire for manifestation. They seek to express subjective thoughts and emotions into objective forms.

4. *Archangels and Kerubim of the four Fire subquadrants.* These Angels are characterized by their desire to purify human nature. They seek purification by fire of all the lower human character traits.

THE LESSER ANGELS

There are 64 Lesser Angels of the Watchtowers. Beneath the horizontal bar of each Calvary Cross are sixteen squares (four letters across separated by the vertical bar of the Cross, and four letters down). These are the names of the four Lesser Angels of each respective subquadrant, the first being somewhat more important than the other three.

I. Air.
1. Air of Air: KZNS, TOTT, SIAS, FMND
2. Water of Air: O^Y_vUB, PAOK, RBNH, DIR^h
3. Earth of Air: ABMO, NAKO, OKNM, SHAL
4. Fire of Air: AKKA, NP^U_AT, OTOI, PMOX

II. Water.
1. Air of Water: T^O_AKO, NHDD, ^F_PAAX, SAI^Z_X
2. Water of Water: $^M_I{}^A_{Nu}$GM, I^L_AOK, $VS^X_S{}^Y_N{}^L_H$, RV^L_KI
3. Earth of Water: PAKO, NDZN, ^R_IIPO, XRNH
4. Fire of Water: XPKN, VASA, DAPI, R^N_AIL

III. Earth.
1. Air of Earth: AIRA, ORMN, RSNI, IZNR
2. Water of Earth: ^A_OMGG, GBAL, RLMU, IAHL
3. Earth of Earth: OPNA, DOO^P_F, RXAO, AXIR
4. Fire of Earth: MSA^T_L, IABA, IZXP, STIM

IV. Fire.
1. Air of Fire: OPMN, A^P_BST, SKIO, VASG
2. Water of Fire: G^M_NNM, EKOP, AMOX, ^B_VRAP
3. Earth of Fire: DATT, DIOM, OOPZ, RGAN
4. Fire of Fire: ADRE, SISP, PALI, AKAR

The Ruling Lesser Angels.

Each of the 64 Lesser Angels has a presiding Angel whose name can be found by prefixing an appropriate letter from the Tablet of Union.

1. **Air (XARP).**
    1. Air of Air: XKZNS, XTOTT, XSIAS, XFMND
    2. Water of Air: AO$^{Y}_{v}$UB, APAOK, ARBNH, ADIR^{h}
    3. Earth of Air: RABMO, RNAKO, ROKNM, RSHAL
    4. Fire of Fire: PAKKA, PNP$^{U}_{A}$T, POTOI, PPMOX

2. **Water (KOMA).**
    1. Air of Water: KT$^{O}_{A}$KO, KNHDD, K$^{F}_{P}$AAX, KSAI$^{Z}_{X}$
    2. Water of Water: O$^{M}_{I}{}^{A}_{Nu}$GM, OI$^{L}_{A}$OK, OVS$^{X\ YL}_{\ S\text{-}NH}$, ORV$^{L}_{k}$I
    3. Earth of Water: MPAKO, MNDZN, M$^{R}_{l}$IPO, MXRNH
    4. Fire of Water: AXPKN, AVASA, ADAPI, AR$^{N}_{A}$IL

3. **Earth (ANTA).**
    1. Air of Earth: AAIRA, AORMN, ARSNI, AIZNR
    2. Water of Earth: N$^{A}_{o}$MGG, NGBAL, NRLMU, NIAHL
    3. Earth of Earth: TOPNA, TDOO$^{P}_{F}$, TRXAO, TAXIR
    4. Fire of Earth: AMSA$^{T}_{L}$, AIABA, AIZXP, ASTIM

4. **Fire (ITOM).**
    1. Air of Fire: IOPMN, IA$^{P}_{B}$ST, ISKIO, IVASG
    2. Water of Fire: TG$^{M}_{N}$NM, TEKOP, TAMOX, T$^{B}_{v}$RAP
    3. Earth of Fire: ODATT, ODIOM, OOOPZ, ORGAN
    4. Fire of Fire: MADRE, MSISP, MPALI, MAKAR

Chief Characteristics of the Lesser Angels.

The Lesser Angels and Lesser Ruling Angels of the sixteen subquadrants, are characterized according to their locality as follows:

1. *Angels of the four Air subquadrants.* These Angels assist in purifications. They can help free one from illusion, diseases, ignorance and other karmic afflictions by an occult process of sublimation.

2. *Angels of the four Water subquadrants.* These Angels assist in polarizations. They can help make needed changes in one's character or life-style, and can orient one toward a better future.

3. *Angels of the four Earth subquadrants.* These Angels assist in manifestations. They can help one to express inherent inner divinity in daily life.

4. *Angels of the four Fire subquadrants.* These Angels assist in transmutations. They can help to disperse the lower elements of the human nature such as egotism, fear, hate, pride and so on.

THE DEMONS OF THE WATCHTOWERS

Three-lettered names of 128 separate Demons can be found by using pairs of letters, from the sixteen squares under the Calvary Cross, together with an appropriate letter from the Tablet of Union. The names of each Lesser Angel consists of two pairs of letters. Each of these pairs is the base of a name of a Demon or elemental. The third letter is the prefix to the Lesser Angels, from the Tablet of Union.

For example, in the subquadrant Air of Air, eight Demon names are:

XKZ	XNS
XTO	XTT
XSI	XAS
XFM	XND

Another example: In the subquadrant Water of Earth, the eight Demon names are:

NAM	NGG
NGB	NAL
NRL	NMU
NIA	NHL

THE CALLS: WHEN TO USE THEM

Dee and Kelly constructed eighteen Calls, or Keys, to be used for either invocations or for traveling in the Spirit Vision. These are rather cumbersome sentences to be recited out loud, prior to any magical operations involving the Angels and Aethyrs.

Actually there is a total of 49 Calls. The first is usually numbered 0 and is without words. This Key makes the mind empty of all thoughts, much like the Samadhi of Yoga. It is used to invoke or travel to the highest formless levels beyond the first Aethyr and as such would only be used by the most advanced Adepts.

A single Call is used for all thirty Aethyrs. The only change necessary is to insert the name of the appropriate Aethyr being addressed. In the Call, this name is usually left blank until filled in by a magician as needed.

This leaves eighteen Calls usually numbered one through eighteen. The specific rules governing their use are given in Table VII.

Example 1. To invoke (or visit) any Archangel, recite Call 1 then 2.

Example 2. To invoke (or visit) any Ruling Lesser Angel whose first letter is from the line NANTA (but not the "N", which is only used for Archangels) of the Tablet of Union, recite Call 1, then 2 and then 5.

Example 3. To invoke (or visit) any Angel from the sub-quadrant Air of Air, recite only Call 3.

Example 4. To invoke (or visit) any Angel from the sub-quadrant Water of Fire, recite Call 6 and then 17.

TABLE VII. WHEN TO USE THE EIGHTEEN CALLS

Call No.	When To Use Call
1	Use first for all angels associated with the Tablet of Union.
2	Use second for all Archangels of EHNB of the Tablet of Union as well as for all other angels.
3	Use third for all Ruling Lesser Angels of (E)XARP. Use first for Lesser Angels of the Watchtower of Air. Use first (only) for all angels of Air of Air beginning with IDOIGO.
4	Use third for all Ruling Lesser Angels of (H)KOMA. Use first for all Lesser Angels of the Watchtower of Water. Use first (only) for all angels of Water of Water beginning with NELAPR.
5	Use third for all Ruling Lesser Angels of (N)ANTA. Use first for all Lesser Angels of the Watchtower of Earth. Use first (only) for all angels of Earth of Earth beginning with ABALPT.
6	Use third for all Ruling Lesser Angels of (B)ITOM. Use first for all Lesser Angels of the Watchtower of Fire. Use first (only) for all angels of Fire of Fire beginning with RZIONR.
7	Use second for all angels of Water of Air beginning with LLAKZA.
8	Use second for all angels of Earth of Air beginning with AIAOAI.
9	Use second for all angels of Fire of Air beginning with AOVRRZ.
10	Use second for all angels of Air of Water beginning with OBGOTA.
11	Use second for all angels of Earth of Water beginning with MALADI.
12	Use second for all angels of Fire of Water beginning with IAAASD.
13	Use second for all angels of Air of Earth beginning with ANGPOI.
14	Use second for all angels of Water of Earth beginning with ANAEEM.
15	Use second for all angels of Fire of Earth beginning with OPMNIR.
16	Use second for all angels of Air of Fire beginning with NOALMR.
17	Use second for all angels of Water of Fire beginning with VADALI.
18	Use second for all angels of Earth of Fire beginning with VOLXDO.

THE EIGHTEEN CALLS TO BE RECITED

The eighteen Calls are written in flowery and rather obscure language. The beginner is very apt to "not see the forest for the trees" in this morass of colorful verbiage. The real purpose of these Calls is to place the mind in a proper receptive state. This is difficult to accomplish, however, when the wording is impossible to comprehend. To avoid this problem for the beginner, each call has been slightly revised for simplicity. The actual Calls, as given by Crowley, are contained in Appendix A. They are for the more daring magician. Accompanying each Call is Crowley's version of the Enochian. The student is encouraged to wade through these and determine for himself, by experience, which version has the best results. Remember, Enochian words are like mantras; they have definite physical vibratory effects as well as emotional and mental effects. But in themselves, they are simply devices used by the magician in order to manifest his will.

1. The First Call.

"I rule over you," declares the God of Justice. His power is exalted above the torment of the world. In his hands, the Sun is like a sword and the Moon is like an all-consuming fire. He measures your clothing material among the available substances and draws you together like the palms of my hands. [Furthermore he says:] "I have decorated your seats with the Fire of Gathering, and have beautified your garments with admiration. I have made a law to govern the Holy Ones, and have delivered a Rod to you, with the Ark of Knowledge. Moreover, you have lifted up your voices and sworn obedience and faith to Him who lives and triumphs, whose beginning is not, and whose end cannot be, who shines like a flame in the center of your palaces, and who rules among you as the balance of righteousness and truth."

[The magician addresses the appropriate Angels and says:]

Move therefore, and show yourselves! Unveil the mysteries of your creation! Be friendly to me, because I am a servant of this same God, a true worshipper of the Highest.

Notes to the First Call. Here the God of Justice is Karma. The pronoun "you" refers throughout to the Angels of the Tablet of Union being addressed by the Call.

2. The Second Call.

Can the winged winds understand your wonderous voices? You are the Second of the First. Burning flames outline you when I speak your names. I will treat you like cups for a wedding, or like beautiful flowers in the Chamber of Righteousness. Your feet are stronger than the barren stone, and your voices are mightier than many winds. You are becoming like a building which does not exist save in the Mind of the All-Powerful.

[The magician addresses the appropriate Angels and says:]

The First commands you to arise and to move therefore toward his servant. Show yourselves in power, and make me a strong Seer-of-things, because I am of Him who lives forever.

Notes to the Second Call. Here the "First" refers to the God of Justice (*i.e.* Karma) of the first Call. He is above the Angels of the Tablet of Union and therefore they are "Second."

3. The Third Call.

"Behold," declares your God, "I am a circle on whose hands stand Twelve Kingdoms. Six of these are seats of life, the rest are like sharp Sickles, or like the Horns of Death. Because of this, the creatures of Earth live or die only in my own hands, which sleep and then rise again."

"In the beginning I made you stewards, and placed you in the twelve seats of govenment. I gave every one of you an appropriate level of power over the 456 true ages of time. My intent was that from the highest vessels and the fartherest corners of your governments, you might work my Power and pour down the fires of life and multiply upon the earth. Thus you have become the skirts of justice and truth."

[The magician addresses the appropriate Angels and says:]

In the name of this same God, lift yourselves up, I say. Behold, His mercies flourish, and His Name has become mighty among us. In Him we say, move, and descend. Apply yourselves to us as you would to partakers of His Secret Wisdom in your creation.

Notes to the Third Call. Here the "Twelve Kingdoms" are the twelve houses of the Zodiac. Here again the pronoun "you" refers throughout to the Angels being addressed. The Enochian word MIKA, which means "mighty" or "powerful", has the numerical value by Gematria of 456. Also, 456 can be reduced, by a process called "Aiq Bkr" or the Qabalah of Nine Chambers, to $4 + 5 + 6 = 15$, where 15 is the number for the word TA, meaning "correspondence."

4. The Fourth Call.

I place my feet in the South, and look about me and say, "Are not the thunders of increase numbered 33, and do these not rule in the Second Angle? I have placed 9639 servants under them. None have yet numbered them, but One. In them, the Second Beginnings of Things exists and grows strong. They are the successive Numbers of Time. Their powers are like those of the first 456.

"Arise, you Sons of Pleasure, and visit the Earth. I am the Lord your God, who is, and who lives forever."

[The magician addresses the appropriate Angels and says:]

In the name of the Creator, move and show yourselves as pleasant deliverers, and praise Him among the sons of men.

Notes to the Fourth Call. Here the "Second Angle" is Water. Thirty-three is the numerical value of L-BESZ which means "the first (*i.e.* primordial) matter." The direction *South,* can be taken as the direction inward, which is to say toward the spiritual. The number 9636 reduces to $9 + 6 + 3 + 6 = 27$ and $2 + 7 = 9$. Also 33 is equivalent to 456 because $3 + 3 = 6$, and $4 + 5 + 6 = 15$ and $1 + 5 = 6$. The number 9 is the value of the letter T which means the same thing as the word TA ("likeness" or "correspondence").

5. The Fifth Call.

Mighty sounds have entered into the Third Angle, and have become like olives on the Olive Mount. They look with gladness upon the Earth, and dwell in the brightness of the heavens like continual Comforters. On them I have fastened 19 Pillars of Gladness and gave them vessels to water the Earth together with her creatures. They are the brothers of the First and Second. They have begun their own seats and have decorated them with 69,636 ever-burning lamps. Their numbers are as the Beginnings, the Ends, and the Contents of Time.

[The magician addresses the appropriate Angels and says:]

Therefore come and obey the purpose of your creation. Visit us in peace and comfort. Perfect us as receivers of your mysteries. Why? Because our Lord and Master is the All-One.

Notes to the Fifth Call. The "Third Angle" refers to any of the four earth subquadrants. Nineteen is the number for BAG, the name of the 28th Aethyr, and $19 \times 7 = 133$, which is the number for VTI, the name of the 25th Aethyr. The number

19 is also the square root of 361, the number for IKH, the name of the 11th Aethyr. Also, $69,636 = 6 + 9 + 6 + 6 + 3 + 6 = 30$ and $30 = 3 + 0 = 3$, i.e. the Third Angle.

6. The Sixth Call.

The spirits of the Fourth Angle are nine who are mighty in the Firmament of Waters, who the First has planted as a torment to the wicked and a garland to the righteous. He gave them fiery darts to protect the earth, and 7699 continual workmen, whose courses visit the earth with comfort and who are in government and continuance like the Second and the Third.

[The magician addresses the appropriate Angels and says:]

Therefore listen to my voice. I have spoken of you, and I have advanced you in power and presence. Your works shall be a song of honor, and the praise of your God shall be in your creation.

Notes to the Sixth Call. The "Fourth Angle" refers to any of the four fire subquadrants. The number 9 occurs throughout these Calls. This is the occult number for the circumference of a circle (360 degrees reduces to 9) and therefore any outward or objective quantity. The number 7699 reduced to $7 + 6 + 9 + 9 = 31$, an important number in Qabalism, and $3 + 1 = 4$, i.e. the Fourth Angle.

7. The Seventh Call.

The East is a House of Virgins who sing praises among the flames of the first glory. There the Lord opened his mouth, and they became 28 living dwellings wherein the strength of man rejoices. They are clothed with ornaments of brightness, and they work wonders on all creatures. Their kingdoms and continuance are like the Third and

Fourth; strong towers and places of comfort, the seats of mercy and continuance.

[The magician addresses the appropriate Angels and says:]

O you Servants of Mercy, move and appear! Sing praises to the Creator, and be mighty among us, so that this remembrance will give power, and our strength will grow strong in our Comforter.

Notes to the Seventh Call. The East is the direction of the Watchtower of Air. Twenty-eight is the number for the word BALT which means "justice." Here the angels are associated with mercy and comfort. Also, 28 = 2 + 8 = 10, and 10 = 1 + 0 = 1, i.e. the First Watchtower.

8. The Eighth Call.

The Midday, where the First is like the Third Heaven, is made of 26 Hyacinthine Pillars. Here the Elders become strong. "I have prepared them for my own righteousness," declared the Lord, whose long continuance is like a shield to the Stooping Dragon, and like the harvest of a widow. How many are there who remain in the Glory of the Earth, who live, and who shall not see Death until the House falls and the Dragon sinks?

[The magician addresses the appropriate Angels and says:]

Come away! The Thunders have spoken. Come away! The Crowns of the Temple and the Robe of Him who is, was, and will be crowned, are divided. Come forth! Appear, to the terror of the Earth and our comfort, and to the comfort of such who are prepared.

Notes to the Eighth Call. "The First is like the Third Heaven" refers to the subquadrant Earth (third) of Air (first). Twenty-six is the number for the word BAHAL meaning "to shout" or "to cry out." Also 26 is half of 52, the number of QAA, "creation." Twenty-six is also the Enochian number for DAATH, the hidden *Eleventh* Sephiroth. Also 26 = 2 + 6 = 8, i.e. the Eighth Call. Here the Angels are associated with a culmination of endurance. The "Stooping Dragon" is Apophrassz (the Apophis or Apep of the Egyptians).

9. The Ninth Call.

A mighty guard of fire, with two-edged swords flaming, and with eight Vials of Wrath for two times and a half, and with wings of wormwood and with marrow of salt, have set their feet in the West. They are measured with their 9996 ministers. These gather up the moss of the Earth like the rich man gathers up his treasure. Cursed are they who have iniquities. In the eyes of those with iniquities are millstones greater than the Earth and from their mouths run seas of blood. The heads of the Guard of Fire are covered with diamonds, and upon their hands are marble stones. Happy is he upon whom they frown not, because the Lord of Righteousness rejoices in them.

[The magician addresses the appropriate Angels and says:]

Come away, but without your Vials, because the time is such that requires comfort.

Notes to the Ninth Call. The references to Fire of Air are clear here. According to the Zodiac correspondence, West is the direction of Air. Eight Vials for two times and a half: 8 + 8 + 4 = 20. Also, 9996 = 9 + 9 + 9 + 6 = 33, and 33 = 3 + 3 = 6. Furthermore, 20 + 6 = 26. Both 20 and 26 are Enochian numbers for DAATH, the Dark Sephiroth. Here the Angels are clearly purgative.

10. The Tenth Call

The Thunders of Judgment and Wrath are numbered, and are contained in the North, in the likeness of an Oak whose branches are 22 nests of lamentation and weeping which are stored up for the Earth. These burn night and day, and vomit out the heads of scorpions and live sulphur mingled with poison. These are the Thunders that, 5678 times in the twenty-fourth part of a moment, roar with a hundred mighty earthquakes and a thousand times as many surges. They rest not, neither do they know any time here. One rock brings forth a thousand, just as the heart of man brings forth his thoughts. Woe! Woe! Woe! Woe! Woe! Yea, Woe to the Earth, because her iniquity is, was, and shall be great.
[The magician addresses the appropriate Angels and says:]
Come away! But not your mighty sounds.

Notes to the Tenth Call. According to the Zodiac correspondence, North is the direction of Water and these "Thunders" and "mighty sounds" occur in air (*i.e.* Air of Water). The "22 nests" are the trumps of the Tarot, the paths between the Sephiroth on the Tree of Life. $5678 = 5 + 6 + 7 + 8 = 26$, and $2 + 6 = 8$, the occult number for spiral cycles. Here the Angels are associated with the turmoil and flux of powerful karmic forces.

11. The Eleventh Call.

The mighty Seat groaned, and there were five Thunders that flew into the East, and then an eagle spoke and cried aloud, "Come away!" And then they gathered themselves together and became the House of Death, which is measured, and they were like those whose number is 31.
[The magician addresses the appropriate Angels and says:]
Come away! I have prepared a place for you. Therefore,

move and show yourselves. Unveil the mysteries of your creation. Be friendly to me, because I am a servant of this same God, a true worshipper of the Highest.

Notes to the Eleventh Call. East is the direction of Air. Also, "Thunders" and "eagle" suggest air. However, all of the air has "come away" leaving Earth of Water which is "the House of Death." Thirty-one is the number for the word BESZ, "matter." It should also be noted that Death is the 13th path on the Tree of Life and 13 is the reverse of 31 (both reduce to 4, the occult number for solidity and firmness which characterize the element Earth). Here opportunity and possiblility give way to fatality which is a kind of death (in an occult sense, death is stagnation). Also, if 5 (the number of Thunders) is added to 31, the sum reduces to 9 (see the note to the Fourth Call).

12. The Twelfth Call.

O you who range in the South, and who are the 28 Lanterns of Sorrow, bind up your girdles, and visit us. Bring down your 3663 servants so that the Lord may be magnified. His name among you is Wrath.

[The magician addresses the appropriate Angels and says:]

Move I say, and show yourselves! Unveil the mysteries of your creation. Be friendly to me, because I am a servant of this same God, a true worshipper of the Highest.

Notes to the Twelfth Call. South is the direction of the element Fire. Twenty-eight is the number for the word BALT which means "justice." Also, 28 reduces to 1. 3663 = 3 + 6 + 6 + 3 = 18, and 18 = 1 + 8 = 9. The sum of 3663 and 28 reduces to 1, the occult number for unity. Sorrow and wrath accompany the purification by fire only for the unprepared.

13. The Thirteenth Call.

O Swords of the South, who have 42 eyes to stir up the Wrath of Sin, who make men drunken who are empty; Behold, the Promise of God, and His Power which is called among you a bitter sting.

[The magician addresses the appropriate Angels and says:]

Move and appear! Unveil the mysteries of your creation, because I am a servant of this same God, a true worshipper of the Highest.

Notes to the Thirteenth Call. The "Swords of the South" can also be considered "spiritual swords" because South is the direction of the spiritual. The "Promise of God" refers to the Air of Earth, the region of possible manifestations. Forty-two is the number of the word ELZAP which means "way" or "course." Also, $42 = 4 + 2 = 6$, the occult number for the principle of animation and physical nature. The Angels called here can help hasten the growth of one's karmic seeds.

14. The Fourteenth Call.

O Sons of Fury, O Children of the Just One, who sit upon 24 seats, who vex all creatures of the Earth with age, and who have 1636 servants under you; Behold, the Voice of God, the promise of Him who is called among you, Fury or Extreme Justice.

[The magician addresses the appropriate Angels and says:]

Move and show yourselves! Unveil the mysteries of your creation. Be friendly to me, because I am a servant of this same god, a true worshipper of the Highest.

Notes to the Fourteenth Call. Here the Angels are associated with fury and turmoil, albeit karmic. Twenty-four is the number for LEA, the name of the 16th Aethyr, and PAZ, the 4th Aethyr. Also, $24 \times 2 = 48$ where 48 is the number for

POP, the 19th Aethyr, and LOE, the 12th Aethyr. All of these Aethyrs are related through the number 24. Also the word TAFA, "poison" is 24. This number reduces to 6 (2 + 4 = 6). 1636 = 1 + 6 + 3 + 6 = 16, one-third of 48. Also 1 + 6 = 7, the occult number for completeness. Seven is also half of fourteen, the number of this Call. The sum of 24 and 1636 reduces to 6 + 7 = 13 and 13 = 1 + 3 = 4, i.e. the Fourth Watchtower, or Earth. These Angels seek change which appears as fury to the unprepared, and justice to the initiated.

15. The Fifteenth Call.

O Governor of the First Flame, under whose wings are 6739 servants, who weaves the Earth with dryness, and who knows the Great Name of "Righteousness," and the Seal of Honor.

[The magician addresses the appropriate Angels and says:]

Move and appear! Unveil the mysteries of your creation. Be friendly to me, because I am a servant of this same God, a true worshipper of the Highest.

Notes to the Fifteenth Call. The "First Flame" relates this Call to the Element of Fire, and "weaving the Earth with dryness" relates it to Earth (*i.e.* to Fire of Earth). 6739 = 6 + 7 + 3 + 9 = 25 and 25 is the number for BESZ, "matter." Also, 2 + 5 = 7 to show that the servants of this Call are similar to those in the 14th Call. These Angels are associated with the manifestation of purity.

16. The Sixteenth Call.

O Second Flame, O House of Justice, who has His beginning in glory, and who comforts the Just, who walks upon the Earth with 8763 feet, and who understands and separates creatures. You are great, like the God of Conquest.

[The magician addresses the appropriate Angels and says:]
Move and appear! Unveil the mysteries of your creation. Be friendly to me, because I am a servant of this same God, a true worshipper of the Highest.

Notes to the Sixteenth Call. The sense of justice and comfort given here characterizes the subquadrant of Air. The "Flame" refers to the element Fire. $8763 = 8 + 7 + 6 + 3 = 24$ (see the 14th Call for this number).

17. The Seventeenth Call.
O Third Flame, whose wings are thorns to stir up vexation, and who has 7336 living lamps going before you, and whose God is "Wrath in Anger."
[The magician addresses the appropriate Angels and says:]
Gird up your loins and listen! Move and appear! Unveil the mysteries of your creation. Be friendly to me, because I am a servant of this same God, a true worshipper of the Highest.

Notes to the Seventeenth Call. The "Flame" refers to the element Fire, and the "stirring up" is a reference to Water. When Water meets Fire, a great disturbance or "vexation" is produced. $7336 = 7 + 3 + 3 + 6 = 19$, and $19 = 1 + 9 = 10 = 1 + 0 = 1$.

18. The Eighteenth Call.
O Mighty Light and burning Flame of Comfort, who unveils the Glory of God to the center of the Earth, and in who the 6332 Secrets of Truth have their abode, and who is called in your kingdom, "Joy" and who is not to be measured.
[The magician addresses the appropriate Angels and says:]
Be a window of comfort to me! Move and appear! Unveil the mysteries of your creation. Be friendly to me,

because I am a servant of this same God, a true worshipper of the Highest.

Notes to the Eighteenth Call. Here Fire of Fire is emphasized, but the secret nature of this *fire* is joy. 6332 = 6 + 3 + 3 + 2 = 14, the number for the word AG meaning "no" or "not." Also 14 = 1 + 4 = 5, the occult number for a mixture of spirit and matter (also the number for man).

HOW TO INVOKE
THE ARCHANGELS AND ANGELS

The Kerubic Angels, Archangels and Lesser Angels are all invoked using the appropriate Calls from Table VII, together with the Pentagram Ritual. Each Angel is attributed to the element of the corresponding Watchtower. The Archangels and Ruling Lesser Angels are attributed to Spirit, the element of the Tablet of Union.

A pentagram has five points and each corresponds to an element, and therefore to one of the Holy Tablets. During the ritual, a pentagram is drawn for a particular Angel or Archangel by beginning it at the appropriate point. The pentagram is shown in Figure 16. The four lower points correspond to the Watchtowers, and above them is Spirit which corresponds to the Tablet of Union.

Figure 16. Pentagram for Invocation and Banishment of Angels and Archangels.

Invocation of Archangels and Angels: Step by Step

A. PREPARATION.
1. Select the Archangel or Angel to be invoked. This will depend upon the motive or purpose for the invocation.
2. Determine the corresponding Watchtower, Angel and Element.
3. Determine and be familiar with the appropriate Calls, from Table VII.
4. Memorize the pronounciation of all names involved. The order of the Enochian Hierarchies is:
    a. Great Holy Name
    b. Great King
    c. Six Seniors
    d. Calvary Cross Angel (six letters)
    e. Calvary Cross Controlling Angel (five letters)
    f. Archangel
    g. Kerubic Angel
    h. Ruling Lesser Angel
    i. Lesser Angel
    j. Demons
5. Consult Figures 16, 17 and 18 to determine the appropriate pentagrams to be drawn.
6. Stand facing the appropriate Watchtower (*i.e.* North, South, East, or West from Figure 8).

B. INVOCATION.
1. Begin by reciting out loud the appropriate Call or Calls in their proper order. Concentration should place the mind in a receptive state, tuned to the vibratory forces of the particular Angel being invoked.
2. Trace a large pentagram in the air with either a magic wand or rod.
    a. Begin at the point of the pentagram shown in Figures 17 and 18 depending upon the corre-

sponding element. There are two pentagrams for the Tablet of Union, one for E and B (both are active) and another for H and N (both are passive).

b. Trace the pentagram in a single unbroken line. Begin in the direction shown in the figures by the arrow and continue until returning to the starting point.

c. Imagination is important here. As the magician traces the lines in the air, he imagines that a pentagram is actually being drawn. He must be able to see it very clearly in his mind. The color of this psychic construction is as follows:

If the starting point is:	Then the color of the pentagram is:
Spirit (E,B)	bright purple
Spirit (H,N)	deep purple
Air	sky blue
Water	sea green
Earth	amber
Fire	bright fiery vermillion

d. To further tax the imagination, after any pentagram is drawn, imagine the following symbol at the center of it, shining with the same color:

> Spirit
> Air
> Water
> Earth
> Fire

3. As a general rule, pronounce the Holy Name while tracing the pentagram and the Great King's name while constructing the inner symbol. Then pronounce

INVOCATION   BANISHMENT

   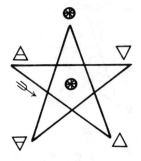

Pentagrams for Invocation and Banishment of Angels
and Archangels Whose Names Begin with the E(XARP)
of Air and the B(ITOM) of Fire.

INVOCATION   BANISHMENT

   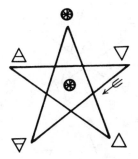

Pentagrams for Invocation and Banishment of Angels
and Archangels Whose Names Begin with the H(KOMA)
of Water and the N(ANTA) of Earth.

Figure 17. Pentagrams for the Element of Spirit.

INVOKING   BANISHING

Figure 18. Invoking and Banishing Pentagrams for Angels and Archangels of the Four Elements.

the names of all six Seniors while concentrating on the pentagram.

4. Continue calling out the names of the angelic hierarchy in their proper sequence until naming the Angel to be invoked. While speaking outwardly, the magician vibrates the name inwardly, mentally filling the universe with it. If done properly, this will have the effect of clearly visualizing the locality of the invoked Angel and his exact relationship with the Watchtower. In other words, it will establish a psycho-magnetic link between the magician and the Angel.

5. If successful, he will appear in the pentagram in some form and will converse with the magician. If partially successful, the magician may catch an idea or thought from him.

6. Success or failure is not measured by requiring that an Angel physically jump out of the Aether at the magician. It is measured only by the degree in achievement of the original motive. Success or failure may not be known for days or even months after the operation.

C. BANISHMENT.

1. Every Angel invoked, must be properly banished after the operation. If unsure whether the invocation was successful or not, use the banishment ritual anyway. It is a psychological necessity to banish these foreign impulses and forces from one's consciousness lest they influence one unconsciously (which is a form of possession).

2. To banish an Archangel or Angel back to his region, simply make another pentagram in reverse, as shown in Figures 17 and 18.

3. As the banishing pentagram is drawn, imagine that the colored lines previously traced are being erased (this may take some practice at first). Imagine that the

central symbol disappears simultaneously. When the banishing pentagram has been drawn properly, the magician will no longer see any pentagram at all. He should feel that a great distance once again separates him from the Angel.

An Invocation of a Lesser Angel.

Suppose, for an example, one would like to increase his capacity for knowledge. Perhaps he has a poor memory, or is slow to learn new things. In order to ease this problem, he decides to call on the assistance of ABMO, the highest of the Lesser Angels in the subquadrant Earth of Air.

As part of his preparation, the magician finds that ABA can mean "to bend" or "to come down" and that OM means "knowledge" or "understanding." AB-OM can thus mean "the coming down of knowledge," and the Angel, AB-MO, (where MO is an anagram for OM) is "he who brings down knowledge." He also calculates the gematric value of ABMO to be 131 and uses this number to find an equivalent Enochian word or phrase. He knows that he will be working on the Watchtower of Air, so he reviews the Governing Angels of this quadrant and the two pentagrams to be used (one for invoking the other for banishing).

The magician begins by casting aside all distracting thoughts and concerns. He should be alone, or at least without distractions or interruptions. Once such operations begin, any interruption could be disastrous.

The magician stands with arms outstretched facing the East and recites Call no. 3 and then Call no. 8. The meanings of these Calls must be clear. Their symbolism should lead to a vibratory feeling for the subquadrant Earth of Air.

Then the magician speaks the Holy Name, *Oh-roh Ee-bah Ah-oh-zod-pee* and vibrates it in his mind while tracing a large light blue Air Pentagram. He should be able to see the blue pentagram shining in the air before him.

He then sees a light blue symbol for Air (△) in the center of the pentagram while he simultaneously vibrates the five-syllabled name of *Bah-tah-ee-vah-heh*, "he whose voice seems to have wings."

As he looks at the completed pentagram, he slowly vibrates the names of the six Seniors:

> Hab-bee-oh-roh
> Ah-ah-oh-zodah-eefeh
> Heh-teh-noh-rah-dah
> Ah-ha-oh-zodah-pee
> Ah-veh-toh-tah-rah
> Hee-poh-teh-gah

By now the magician should be in good rapport with the Watchtower of Air. A psycho-magnetic link should be clearly established. He is now ready to proceed to the proper subquadrant. He begins by saying:

> "Ahee-ah-oh-ahee, who stands upright at the great Cross, be within me, and grant my request.
>
> Ohee-ee-ee-teh, who expands outward to control the mighty Cross, be within me and without me, and grant my request.
>
> O Mighty Archangel, Eh-ten-beh-rah, who guards over the Earth of Air, manifest my request; make my inner desire for knowledge to be an outer reality.
>
> O mighty and merciful Kerubic Angel, Ten-beh-rah, may my inherent capacity for knowledge be made manifest in this life. O Ten-beh-rah, may a balance be made between ignorance and wisdom.
>
> O kindly presiding Angel, Rah-beh-moh, may knowledge of all things come easily to me."

The magician has now worked his way down to the Angel who is to be invoked, ABMO. Consciousness which was first expanded in all directions (*i.e.* blank), has been guided to the great Watchtower of Air in the east, and then to the subquadrant Earth of Air, and then to the specific squares of that subquadrant where the Lesser Angel ABMO dwells. All the while the original goal is kept firmly in mind and the Air Pentagram still sparkles in the air before the magician's eyes. He is now ready to invoke ABMO:

> "O Ah-bem-oh, who governs over the three Lesser Angels Nah-koh, Oh-ken-em, and Ess-hah-el; assist me!
>
> O Ah-bem-oh, whose number is one hundred and thirty-one, attend me!
>
> You are ETHAMZA (Eteh-ahm-zodah) MAD-BESZ (Em-ah-deh Bess-zod) (*i.e.* "you are hidden by the God of Matter." Both of these equal 131).
>
> Ah-bem-oh, Ah-bem-oh, come to me. Make the ASr of Knowledge to be the earth of intelligence for me. Help me to fully realize my inherent ability to learn and to retain what is learned. May I be made firm in knowledge even as you are earthed in Air.
>
> Ah-bem-oh, assist me!

Now the magician should feel the airy nature of knowledge becoming a solid fact within himself. He imagines ABMO in the pentagram showering forth his ability to manifest the capacity for knowledge. He is now one who can learn easily and remember facts over long periods of time. His own inherent ability will now surely be enhanced.

In gratitude to ABMO, he now banishes the Angel with a banishing Air Pentagram. ABMO thus returns to the Watchtower of Air in the East; the pentagram leaves his sight.

A successful outcome here is likely because the magician has requested that an inherent ability (*i.e.* inherent in man) be made manifest in this life. The Angel was not asked to perform an impossible mission. He was asked only to assist the magician to make a desired psychological change within himself in accordance with the Great Work. Enochian Magic is extremely powerful in this regard.

RELATIONSHIP OF THE WATCHTOWERS
TO THE TREE OF LIFE

Both Crowley and the Golden Dawn sought to show a correspondence between the Enochian system and the Hebrew system of the Qabalah and its Tree of Life. The Tree of Life consists of ten Sephiroth, globes of splendor, from Kether the most spiritual down to Malkuth, our Earth and the most material. These globes are situated as shown in Figure 19. There are 22 paths connecting these globes. These paths are each represented by one of the trump cards of the Tarot. Figure 19 also shows the matching Enochian letters.

It can be seen from this, and from the data contained in Table II, that an exact match is not possible. Three paths have two letters each, while three paths (Sun, Tower, and Fortune) have none. Crowley states (in *The Vision and the Voice*) that the Aethyrs approach the Tree of Life, but are nowhere identical. Nevertheless, a fairly good correspondence can be made using the Abyss as a common reference point for the two systems. The dark and hidden Sephiroth of Daath corresponds tolerably well with the tenth Aethyr.

The Calvary Crosses of the Watchtowers bear a direct correspondence with the Sephiroth, as shown in Figure 20. Each Calvary Cross in the four Fire subquadrants, represent the Sephiroth in the Atziluth World. Each Cross in the four Water subquadrants, correspond to the Sephiroth in the Briah World. Each Cross in the Air subquadrants, the Yetzirah World, and the four Earth subquadrants, the Assiah World. These four worlds or cosmic planes each contain ten Sephiroth according to Qabalistic tradition.

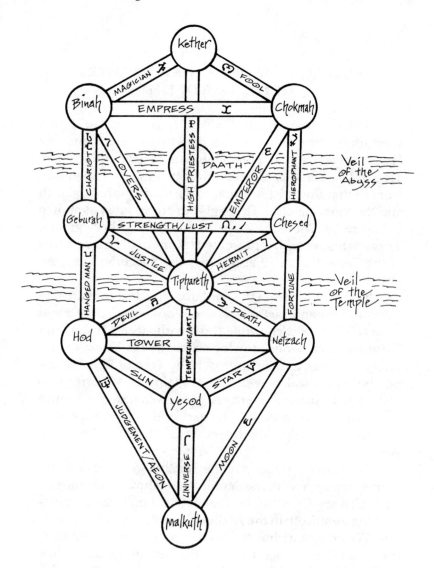

Figure 19. Enochian Correspondence with the Qabalistic Tree of Life.

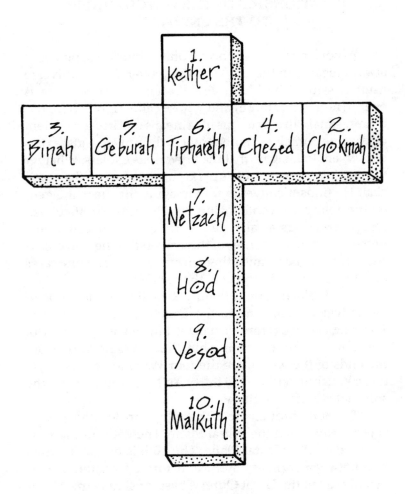

**Figure 20. Correspondence Between the Calvary Cross and
the Ten Sephiroth.**

RELATIONSHIP OF THE WATCHTOWERS
TO THE UNIVERSE

According to ancient occult philosophy, each person is always located in the center of the universe. The universe itself is said to be like a circle whose circumference is everywhere (*i.e.* infinite) and whose center is nowhere (*i.e.* infinitesimal). In magic, this idea means that it is convenient to imagine ourselves at the center of the universe just as it is convenient to imagine that the universe is endless. Whether these things be so or not, is of no consequence to the magician. He finds it convenient to imagine that he is the geometric point at the center of infinity. He finds no difficulty in regarding others as also geometric points, or consciousness-centers, at the center of the universe. If the universe is considered to be infinite, then virtually any point one cares to select can be said to lay at the center.

The Tablet of Union (Figure 9) is the central region of the universe, according to the Enochian magical system. The magician therefore visualizes himself at the center of the Tablet of Union. Around him, like walls rising up from the ends of the world, are the four Watchtowers. Around these Watchtowers are the thirty Aethyrs rising up into the spiritual realms of infinity.

The 30th through the 27th Aethyrs are located in what is generally called the Astral Plane. The 26th through the 11th are on the Mental Plane. The 10th is on the dividing line between formless spirit and formed matter. This is usually called the Great Outer Abyss, or simply the Abyss. The higher Aethyrs, 9th through the 1st, are spiritual.

Figure 21 is a diagram of this relationship. The magician visualizes himself standing between the "O" of HKOMA and the "N" of NANTA at the center of the universe. In this way, the quadrants, Aethrys, Angels, and so forth can become very real and meaningful. Mind traveling to certain squares, subquadrants or Aethyrs, is equivalent to traveling through one's own universe. Figure 21 must not be taken too literally by the beginner. It is a diagram only. Actually the Watchtowers and Aethyrs overlap to a large extent. In fact, the Governors of the Aethyrs are named in the letters of the Watchtowers and through a study of these names, the actual relationships can become known.

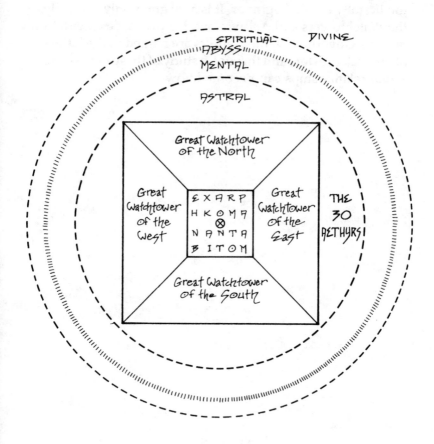

Figure 21. The Magician (⊗) Standing at the Center of the Universe.

TRAVELING IN THE SPIRIT VISION: GENERAL

When Angels are invoked, there must be a reason or motive behind the invocation which relates to the nature of the Angel. Invocations are therefore generally limited in scope. They are constrained by the motive. Not so is traveling in the *Spirit Vision*.

The ability to consciously leave the physical body and travel mentally through the astral and mental planes is rare, but certainly not unknown. The Golden Dawn referred to such conscious out-of-body experiences as traveling in the Spirit Vision. In truth, whether one actually leaves the physical body in a subtle body and travels in specific directions through the Watchtowers and Aethyrs, or simply uses his imagination tempered by known correspondences, is immaterial to a successful operation. Anyone with a colorful imagination can astral travel, and vice versa.

Just as the Qabalist travels mentally along the paths of the Tarot to the Sephiroth, so the magician here can travel through the four Watchtowers and the thirty Aethyrs.

HOW THE MAGIC WORKS: THREE MAGICAL OPERATIONS WITH SPIRIT VISION

The three most important operations using the Spirit Vision in Enochian Magic are:

a. Skrying in the Spirit Vision
b. Traveling in the Spirit Vision
c. Rising on the Planes or Aethyrs

a. *Skrying in the Spirit Vision.* This is identical with clairvoyance or psychic vision. It is the method most recommended for beginners and should be practiced until proficiency is reached before the other two operations are attempted. Basically, it consists of using *signposts* or known magical symbols and correspondences to "see", with inner vision, the regions or subquadrants so symbolized. The signposts are used to "prime the pump" of the imagination as well as to keep the imagination in check once it begins. Start by meditating on the symbols and signposts pertinent to the operation. Then gradually slide into seeing them mentally rather than physically. The result will be a psychic vision of the region or subquadrant under consideration.

b. *Traveling in the Spirit Vision.* This operation is also known as Astral Traveling or Astral Projection. Here the magician actually separates his consciousness from his physical body and, by a concentration of will, projects himself in either an astral or mental body to the desired Aethyr or Watchtower Square. There he observes the region and its inhabitants directly and returns whenever he so desires. The mechanics of this operation are identical to those for falling asleep and entering a dream. The only real difference is that dreams are subconscious and spontaneous whereas this magical operation is conscious and deliberate. In Astral Projection the magician remains in complete control of any situation that may develop. Unlike skrying, which is two-dimensional, traveling in the Spirit Vision is three-dimensional. The magician actually enters into the region rather than merely visualizing it.

c. *Rising on the Planes or Aethyrs.* This operation is the most advanced and is not recommended for beginners. It should be attempted only after proficiency is established in Astral Projection. The process consists of raising consciousness from the Physical Plane upward (relatively speaking) toward the spiritual realms of the Spiritual Plane and then through them to the Divine Plane. In this sense it is not unlike mysticism and indeed the result is a mystical experience or *samadhi*. The Western Qabalistic Model of the Tree of Life (Sephiroth), the Eastern Gupta-Vidya Model (Globes) and the Enochian Model (Aethyrs) can all be used as structural maps for consciousness during this operation (these models will be described in detail later).

THE TABLET COLORS

Each magician should draw his own Tablets. The colors used should be those prescribed by the Golden Dawn, and presented by Robert Wang in *THE SECRET TEMPLE* (Weiser, New York, 1980). These are shown in Figures 22 and 23. Above each Tablet is the appropriate sigil of the elemental King whose name is found from the Great Seal.

These colored Tablets are important for traveling in the Spirit Vision. They give a sense of orientation and direction, as well as expressing the overall mood or tone of the squares. Familiarization of the territory beforehand, can prevent one from going astray during an operation.

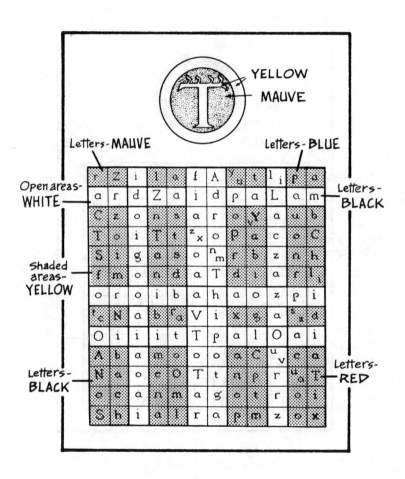

Figure 22. The Colors of the Air Tablet.

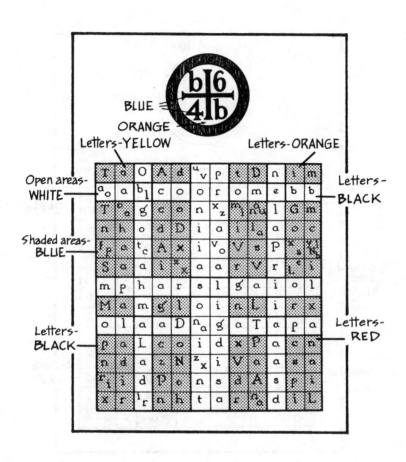

Figure 22a. The Colors of the Water Tablet.

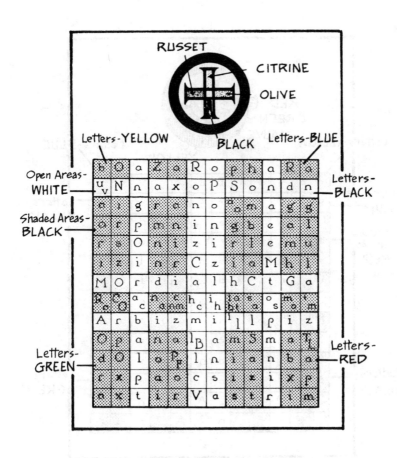

Figure 23. The Colors of the Earth Tablet.

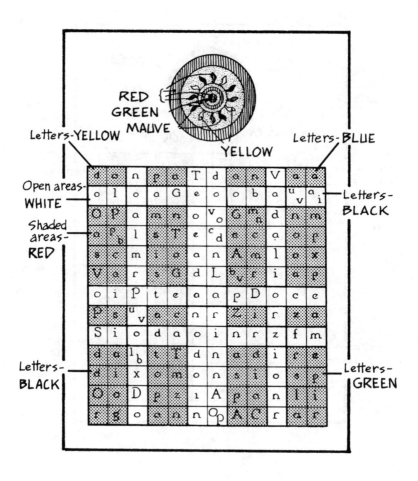

Figure 23a. The Colors of the Fire Tablet.

HOW TO MAKE EACH TABLET SQUARE
INTO A PYRAMID

The Golden Dawn worked out a system whereby each of the Watchtower Squares can be made into a truncated pyramid (This is a pyramid with its top cut off). Figure 24 shows a typical example.

Each pyramid is positioned so that triangle no. 2 faces the top of the Tablet. An elaborate scheme has been devised so that each face of every pyramid has correspondences with planets, Tarot cards, Hebrew letters, and elements. Here, it is sufficient to consider only the elements. The appropriate Enochian letter of the square is placed in the center square which represents the chopped-off top of the pyramid. The similarity between Figure 24 (microcosm) and Figure 21 (macrocosm) should be carefully examined.

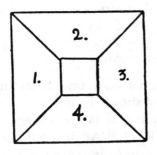

**Figure 24. Top view of a typical Tablet Square
made into a Truncated Pyramid.**

THE SERVIENT SQUARES

Making Pyramids of the Servient Squares.

The Sixteen Servient Squares under the horizontal bar of each Calvary Cross are especially easy to convert into element-affected pryamids. Using the triangular side numbers as shown in Figure 24, the general rules are:

Triangle no. 1 = Element of the Tablet or Watchtower
Triangle no. 2 = Element of ruling file or column
Triangle no. 3 = Element of Subquadrant
Triangle no. 4 = Element of ruling rank or row

To find the appropriate element for any column or row of a Servient Square, use the correspondence shown in Figure 25. The numbers 1 through 4 represent the elements attributed to the row or column indicated. As an example, the Servient Square "R" of BRAP in the Water subquadrant of the Watchtower of Fire (*i.e.* Water of Fire), should be designated,

Triangle no. 1 = Fire
Triangle no. 2 = Earth
Triangle no. 3 = Water
Triangle no. 4 = Air

As an additional aid in understanding these Servient Squares, Figure 26 shows the influences of these elements on any square in terms of its strength and/or weakness. For example, in the "R" of BRAP, it should be clear that Water will be very strong, and Air very weak, while Earth and Fire are about even.

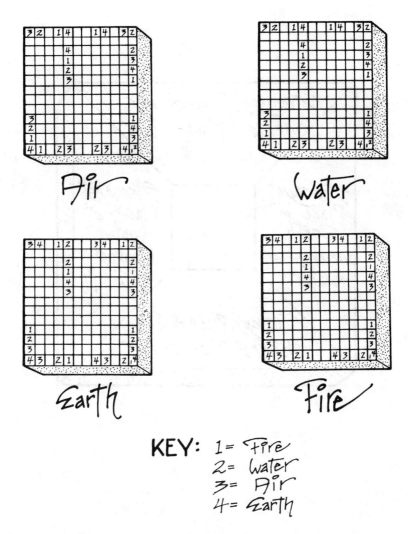

KEY: 1 = Fire
2 = Water
3 = Air
4 = Earth

**Figure 25. Attribution of Elements to the Servient Squares
by column and Row.**

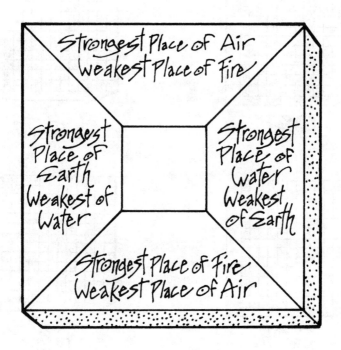

**Figure 26. The Influence of the Elements According
to Placement in the Triangles.**

Egyptian Deities of the Servient Squares

The question of why a magician should make pyramids out of the Servient Squares will now be answered. Each of the Servient Squares in the Watchtowers is ruled by an Egyptian god or goddess. The pyramid, with its four-sided attribution of elements, is used to determine which Egyptian deity presides over each pyramid.

Although technically not part of the Enochian hierarchy, each of these deities can be considered as an additional ruler. However, they usually do not answer to the pentagram or hexagram rituals. For this reason they are seldom invoked but are primarily used when traveling in the Spirit Vision. They are much more familiar to most occultists and magicians than the relatively obscure Enochian Angels. Indeed, Egyptian tradition is the bedrock of western occultism (the Tarot, for example, is the "Book of *Thoth*", the ibis-headed god of wisdom and magic). Their use thus aids the magician to assimilate the general contour of those subtle regions symbolized by each Servient Square. In this way, the Enochian hierarchy itself can easily become more familiar.

The exact Egyptian god or goddess of any Servient Square is found as follows:

1. First convert the Servient Square to a pyramid.
2. Determine the element attributed to each of the four triangular sides.
3. Determine the presiding Egyptian deity from these elements by using Table VIII.

TABLE VIII. EGYPTIAN DEITIES OF THE PYRAMIDS

No.	Elements in Pyramid	Egyptian Ruling Deity
1	One triangle of each element.	Osiris, god of death; ruler of the reincarnation cycle.
2	At least three triangles of Water.	Isis, goddess of nature and magic; ruler of all solidification processes; sister of Nephthys and Set, sister and wife of Osiris.
3a	At least three triangles of Earth.	Horus, hawk-headed god of human evolution; son of Osiris and Isis.
4a	At least three triangles of Fire.	Nephthys, goddess of the esoteric; ruler of all dispersion processes.
5	At least three triangles of Air.	Aroueris, or Ur-Horu, Horus the Elder Horus as humanity matured.
6	Two triangles of Earth and two of Water.	Hathor, cow-goddess, an aspect of Isis as the wife of Horus.
7	Two triangles of Fire and two of Water.	Sothis, goddess of the dog-star Sirius; a form of Isis who initiates each new season.
8	Two triangles of Air and two of Water.	Harpocrates, or Hor-pa-Khrat, Horus the Child, ruler of Silence.
9	Two triangles of Fire and two of Earth.	Apis, god of the emotions and of desire in the form of a bull.
10	Two triangles of Earth and two of Air.	Anubis, dog-headed god of the subtle substances and guide through the after-death state; son of Osiris and Nephthys.
11b	Two triangles of Fire and two of Air.	Bast, cat-headed goddess of darkness and Witchcraft.
12	At least one triangle of Fire, Water and Earth.	Mestha, protector of disembodied consciousness; son of Horus, in the form of a human-headed mummy.
13	At least one triangle of Fire, Water and Air.	Hapi, protector of disembodied consciousness; son of Horus, in the form of an ape-headed mummy.
14	At least one triangle of Earth, Water and Air.	Tuamautel, protector of disembodied consciousness; son of Horus, in the form of a dog-headed mummy.
15	At least one triangle of Earth, Fire and Air.	Qebhsennuf, protector of disembodied consciousness; son of Horus, in the form of a hawk-headed mummy.

a Here nos. 3 and 4 are the reverse of the Golden Dawn attributions. Nephthys is the ruler of the Fire of Dispersion and should control Fire, while Horus is the prototype of man and should rule Earth. The Golden Dawn listing is Either a mistake or a deliberate blind.

b Bast is used where Water is strong and Fire relatively weak. In areas where Fire is strong and Water relatively weak, use the lioness headed goddess Sakhet, ruler of heat and fire, and wife of the god Ptah.

The Sphynx of the Servient Squares.

In addition to an Egyptian deity, each pyramid of the Servient Squares is said to contain a sphynx. This sphynx is a composite of four basic sections and is dependent upon the elements of each triangle. The student can construct a rough likeness of this sphynx as follows:

1. *Head.* The element of Triangle No. 2 determines the head and whether the sphynx has wings:

    Air = Human-headed with wings like an angel
    Water = Eagle- or hawk-headed with wings
    Earth = Bull-headed without wings
    Fire = Lion-headed without wings

2. *Upper Body.* The elements of Triangles 1 and 3 together determine the torso and arms or forelimbs:

    Air = Human torso/limbs plus wings
    Water = Eagle or hawk torso plus wings
    Earth = Bull-like torso/forelimbs
    Fire = Lion-like torso/forelimbs

3. *Lower Body.* The element of Triangle No. 4 determines the lower limbs (and tail for bull, eagle and lion):

    Air = Human legs and feet
    Water = Eagle or hawk legs and tail
    Earth = Bull-like legs and tail
    Fire = Lion-like legs and tail

4. *Sex.* When Air or Fire are emphasized by the triangles the tendency of the sphynx is to be male. When Water or Earth dominate, the tendency is for the sphynx to be female.

Note. The primary purpose of including the sphynx in any pyramid visitation is for a check. If the sphynx seen does not conform to the above signposts, then something is wrong with the Spirit Vision and the operation should be concluded as quickly as possible.

MAKING PYRAMIDS OF
THE GREAT CROSS SQUARES

The 36 squares of the Great Cross of each Watchtower can be converted into pyramids. This is done for meditational purposes as well as to develop signposts for visiting in the Spirit Vision. The Great Cross consists of one row and two columns, as shown in Figure 11 for the Watchtower of Air. Conversion is in accordance with Figure 24 which shows the four trianglar sides of a typical pyramid. The rules which apply are:

Triangle No. 1 = Zodiac Influences
Triangle No. 2 = Element of Spirit
Triangle No. 3 = Planet Influences
Triangle No. 4 = Element of Watchtower

1. Zodiac Influences. The general rules for attributing the Zodiac signs are:
    (a) The four fixed signs are given to the row (*Linea Spiritus Sancti*).
    (b) The four cardinal signs are given to the left-hand column (left side of the *Linea Dei Patris Filiique*).
    (c) The four mutable signs are given to the right-hand column (right side of the *Linea Dei Patris Filiique*).
    (d) Each sign influences three adjacent squares for a total of 36 squares.
The specific rules for Zodiac Influences are:
    a. Great Cross of Air.
        (1) Row. From left to right, three squares each, are: Aquarius, Scorpio, Leo, and then Taurus.
        (2) Left-hand column. From top to bottom, three squares each, are: Libra, Cancer, Aries, and then Capricorn.
        (3) Right-hand column. From top to bottom, three squares each, are: Gemini, Pisces, Sagittarius, and then Virgo.

b. Great Cross of Water.
    (1) Row. From left to right, three squares each, are: Scorpio, Leo, Taurus, and then Aquarius.
    (2) Left-hand column. From top to bottom, three squares each, are: Cancer, Aries, Capricorn, and then Libra.
    (3) Right-hand column. From top to bottom, three squares each, are: Pisces, Sagittarius, Virgo, and then Gemini.

c. Great Cross of Earth.
    (1) Row. From left to right, three squares each, are: Taurus, Aquarius, Scorpio, and then Leo.
    (2) Left-hand column. From top to bottom, three squares each, are: Capricorn, Libra, Cancer, and then Aries.
    (3) Right-hand column. From top to bottom, three squares each, are: Virgo, Gemini, Pisces, and then Sagittarius.

d. Great Cross of Fire.
    (1) Row. From left to right, three squares each, are: Leo, Taurus, Aquarius, and then Scorpio.
    (2) Left-hand column. From top to bottom, three squares each, are: Aries, Capricorn, Libra, and then Cancer.
    (3) Right-hand column. From top to bottom, three squares each, are: Sagittarius, Virgo, Gemini, and then Pisces.

2. Spirit. The second triangle of each pyramid of every Great Cross is assigned the element of Spirit.

3. Planet Influences. Planetary influences are obtained from occult correspondences between the seven sacred planets and the Decans of the Zodiac. These are as follows:

a. Row, from left to right.
        Leo = Saturn, then Jupiter, and then Mars
        Scorpio = Mars, then Sun and then Venus
        Aquarius = Venus, then Mercury and then Moon
        Taurus = Mercury, then Moon, and then Saturn

   b. Left-hand column, top to bottom.
      Aries = Mars, then Sun, and then Venus
      Capricorn = Jupiter, then Mars, and then Sun
      Libra = Moon, then Saturn, and then Jupiter
      Cancer = Venus, then Mercury, and then Moon
   c. Right-hand column, top to bottom.
      Gemini = Jupiter, then Mars, and then Sun
      Pisces = Saturn, then Jupiter, and then Mars
      Sagittarius = Mercury, then Moon, then Saturn
      Virgo = Sun, then Venus, and then Mercury
4. The fourth triangle of each pyramid of every Great Cross is assigned the element of the Watchtower.
5. Color.
   a. Zodiac Influences. These triangles (No. 1) are colored according to type as:
      Fiery Signs (Aries, Leo, Sagittarius) are red
      Watery Signs (Cancer, Scorpio, Pisces) are blue
      Airy Signs (Gemini, Libra, Aquarius) are yellow
      Earthy Signs (Taurus, Virgo, Capricorn) are black
   b. Spirit. All Spirit triangles (No. 2) are white.
   c. Planet Influences. These triangles (No. 3) are colored as:
      Sun and Jupiter are red (Fire)
      Saturn and Mercury are yellow (Air)
      Venus and Moon are black (Earth)
      Mars is blue (Water)
   d. Watchtower. These triangles (No. 4) are colored according to the standard Watchtower colors:
      Air = yellow
      Water = blue
      Earth = black
      Fire = red

Example No. 1.

The square "I" which is the fourth square from the left along the *Linea Spiritus Sancti* in the Great Watchtower of Air (see Figure 4):

Triangle No. 1 = Scorpio, blue (watery)
Triangle No. 2 = Spirit, white
Triangle No. 3 = Mars, blue (watery)
Triangle No. 4 = Air, yellow

Example No. 2.

The square "O" which is the second square from the top along the left side of the *Linea Dei Patris Filiique* in the Great Watchtower of Water (see Figure 5):

Triangle No. 1 = Cancer, blue (watery)
Triangle No. 2 = Spirit, white
Triangle No. 3 = Mercury, yellow (airy)
Triangle No. 4 = Water, blue

Example No. 3.

The square "A" which is the seventh square from the left along the *Linea Spiritus Sancti* in the Great Watchtower of Fire (see Figure 7):

Triangle No. 1 = Aquarius, yellow (airy)
Triangle No. 2 = Spirit, white
Triangle No. 3 = Venus, black (earthy)
Triangle No. 4 = Fire, red

Note: In each Tablet, the two squares of the Linea Spiritus Sancti which cut the Linea Dei Patris Filiique in half are a part of the former, not the latter.

MAKING PYRAMIDS OF THE
SEPHIROTIC CROSS SQUARES

The ten squares of each of the Calvary (Sephirotic) Crosses can be converted into pyramids. The Sephirotic or Calvary Cross is shown in Figure 15. It consists of five horizontal squares and six vertical squares with one square shared by the two bars. Conversion is in accordance with Figure 24. The rules which apply are:

Triangle No. 1   Element of Watchtower
Triangle No. 2   Element of Spirit
Triangle No. 4   Element of Subquadrant
Triangle No. 4   Sephirotic Influence

The first three triangles are self-explanatory and should be colored according to the standard Watchtower/Element colors (Spirit is always white). Triangle No. 4 is determined from Figure 20 for each cross. After finding the correct Sephiroth, use the following correspondences:

No.	Sephiroth	Planet	Color
1	Kether	Jupiter	brilliance
2	Chokmah	Mercury	soft blue
3	Binah	Moon	crimson
4	Chesed	Venus	deep violet
5	Geburah	Mars	orange
6	Tiphareth	Sun	pink rose
7	Netzach	_____	white
8	Hod	_____	white
9	Yesod	_____	white
10	Malkuth	_____	white

Example No. 1.

The first "A" in OLAAD in the subquadrant Earth of Water (see Figure 5). This is also the first "A" in the name MALADI:

Triangle No. 1	Water, blue (Water is weak here)
Triangle No. 2	Spirit, white
Triangle No. 3	Earth, black (Earth is weak here)
Triangle No. 4	Tiphareth (Sun), pink rose (influence here is strong)

Example No. 2.

The first "I" of ILPIZ in the subquadrant of Fire of Earth (see Figure 6):

Triangle No. 1	Earth, black (Earth is strong here)
Triangle No. 2	Spirit, white
Triangle No. 3	Fire, red
Triangle No. 4	Binah (Moon), crimson

Example No. 3.

The "L" in NOALMR in the subquadrant Air of Fire (see Figure 7):

Triangle No. 1	Fire, red
Triangle No. 2	Spirit, white
Triangle No. 3	Air, yellow
Triangle No. 4	Hod, white

MAKING PYRAMIDS OF
THE KERUBIC SQUARES

The Kerubic Squares (four in each subquadrant) are located above the horizontal bar of the Calvary Cross, two on each side of the vertical bar. Conversion is in accordance with Figure 24. The rules which apply are:

Triangle No. 1 = Kerubic Element
Triangle No. 2 = Element of Watchtower
Triangle No. 3 = Kerubic Element
Triangle No. 4 = Element of Subquadrant

Triangle Nos. 2 and 4 are self-explanatory and should be colored according to standard Watchtower/Element colors. Triangle No. 1 is always the same element and color as Triangle No. 3. The correct element to use is found from Figure 25. Use Figure 25 to find the corresponding number (column nos. 1 through 4) of the Kerubic Square desired. Then use the *key* given in Figure 25 to determine the correct Kerubic Element.

Note: The appropriate Kerubic numbers for the subquadrants of Earth and Fire are shown in Figure 25 along the bottom row of each Tablet but are nevertheless the correct Kerubic numbers for the subquadrant. Use only the column numbers, not row numbers.

Example No. 1
The Kerubic Square "S" of PSAK in the subquadrant Earth of Fire:

Triangle No. 1	Air, yellow
Triangle No. 2	Fire, red (Fire is weak here)
Triangle No. 3	Air, yellow
Triangle No. 4	Earth, black

Example No. 2.

The Kerubic Square "A" of PHRA in the subquadrant Water of Earth:

Triangle No. 1	Water, blue (Water is weak here)
Triangle No. 2	Earth, black
Triangle No. 3	Water, blue (Water is strong here)
Triangle No. 4	Water, blue

Example No. 3.

The Kerubic Square "D" of TAAD in the subquadrant Air of Water:

Triangle No. 1	Earth, black (Earth is strong here)
Triangle No. 2.	Water, blue
Triangle No. 3	Earth, black (Earth is weak here)
Triangle No. 4	Air, yellow (Air is weak here)

MAKING PYRAMIDS OF THE
TABLET OF UNION SQUARES

The twenty squares of the Tablet of Union can easily be converted into pyramids. This Tablet is shown in Figure 9. Conversion is in accordance with Figure 24. The rules which apply are:
>Triangle No. 1 = Element of Column
>Triangle No. 2 = Element of Spirit
>Triangle No. 3 = Element of Row
>Triangle No. 4 = Element of Spirit

Example No. 1. The square with letter "E":
>Triangle No. 1 = Spirit, white
>Triangles No. 2 and 4 = Spirit, white
>Triangle No. 3 = Air, yellow

Example No. 2. The square with the letter "X":
>Triangle No. 1 = Air, yellow
>Triangles No. 2 and 4 = Spirit, white
>Triangle No. 3 = Air, yellow

Example No. 3. The square with the letter "P":
>Triangle No. 1 = Fire, red
>Triangles No. 2 and 4 = Spirit, white
>Triangle No. 3 = Air, yellow

Example No. 4. The square with the letter "K":
>Triangle No. 1 = Air, yellow
>Triangles No. 2 and 4 = Spirit, white
>Triangle No. 3 = Water, blue (water is strong here)

TRAVELING IN THE SPIRIT VISION:
STEP BY STEP

A. PREPARATION.
1. Select the area to be visited. This can be either an Aethyr or one of the squares of the four Watchtowers.
2. Determine all known correspondences. These act as guideposts along the way to prevent the imagination from fooling itself or being trapped, or lost. One's imagination will project outwardly one's subconscious fears and tendencies, as in a dream. Traveling in the Spirit Vision is indeed similar to falling asleep. The primary difference is that here one consciously controls events, while dreams are unconscious and spontaneous.
3. Sit or lay quietly and relaxed. It is usually considered best to keep the spine upright and straight. Be this as it may, the goal is to forget the physical body for a time. Twisting oneself into a yogic pretzel is not necessary and can, in fact, be dangerous as well as uncomfortable. The key factor here is to eliminate distractions.

B. THE SPIRIT VISION.
1. Face the appropriate direction.
   a. Use the Zodiac correspondence for the Watchtowers.
   b. No direction is necessary for Aethyrs because they lie in all directions, like concentric spheres.
2. Recite the appropriate Call or Calls.
   a. The Calls for invocations are also used for Spirit Vision.
   b. One Call is used for all of the thirty Aethyrs.
3. Vibrate the names of the corresponding rulers.
   a. The entire appropriate hierarchy should be recited for each square of a Watchtower. Demon names are excluded unless they are specifically being called

(not recommended).

b. Each Aethyr is ruled by three Governors whose names are each vibrated.

c. If entering a Servient Square, call upon the ruling Egyptian deity and observe the sphynx.

4. Feel as though surrounded by the atmosphere desired. Known correspondences should be used until the imagination gives them form and they appear real. As each name is spoken outwardly and vibrated inwardly, the locality of its ruler should be felt and if possible, visualized in the mind.

5. Be fully conscious of the experience. Direct the events as they occur (you will direct them subconsciously anyway). Note any discrepancies or incongruities. Anything that goes against the *signposts* should indicate that something is wrong.

6. Each encounter with an Angel or deity must be dealt with in the same way as an invocation. Show respect and humility, but also show control of the conversation. The advantages to being previously versed in these correspondences are obvious (you can't take a textbook with you).

C. THE RETURN.

1. Normally, the desire to return is alone sufficient to bring one back to the physical body.

2. Vow to remember the experience after returning. Astral experiences, like dreams, are easy to forget or to get distorted when back in the physical body again.

3. Ideally, one should be able to split consciousness so that while one part undergoes experiences in the Watchtowers and Aethyrs, another is fully aware of the physical body and may even be writing down notes or dictating to a scribe. If this is done, a full return is extremely easy.

Signposts for a Spirit Vision: An Example.

Suppose, for an example, that one desires to travel in the Spirit Vision to the Servient Square "D" that is located in the Watchtower of Fire, in the subquadrant Fire of Fire, ruled by the Lesser Angel ADRE. The following *signposts* can be determined beforehand in order to be certain one is on the right track, and to keep the imagination in check:

1. The Holy Name is *Oh-ee-peh Teh-ah-ah Peh-doh-keh*, "He whose name is unchanged from what it was." This name causes turmoil outwardly and doubt inwardly to be a presiding characteristic in this Watchtower.

2. The Great King is *Eh-del-par-nah-ah*, "He who is first to receive the flames." He has a fiery nature, quick to anger and loves change of any kind but especially the dispersion of aggragates into their constituent components.

3. The six Seniors are:

   Ah-ah-eteh-pee-oh   Ah-ah-ped-oh-keh
   Ah-dah-eh-oh-eteh   Ah-noh-doh-ee-neh
   Ah-len-keh-voh-deh   Ah-ree-neh-nah-peh

4. The Angels of the Calvary Cross are:

   RZIONR (Rah-zodee-oh-nar), "He who is in the Waters of the Sun", i.e., he has a solar nature.
   and NRZFM (En-rah-zod-eff-em), "He who visits here six times," i.e., he brings life to this area
   (six is the number for the principle of animation)

5. The Archangel is BIZAZ (Bee-zodah-zod), "He who is with a voice." He aids in the purification of communication (e.g., he purifies thoughts, languages, speech, and the like).

6. The Kerubic Angel is IZAZ (Ee-zodah-zod), "He who is outlined." According to the Golden Dawn, he is "outlined" with a fiery mist. He aids in the purification of definition (e.g., he purifies restrictions and limitations).

7. The Ruling Lesser Angel is MADRE (Em-ah-dareh), "He who would be a god." He can help to make one more godlike.

8. The Lesser Angel is ADRE (Ah-dareh), a "small mountain" or "hill." He can help to increase strength and endurance.

9. The Demon here is named MAD (Em-ah-deh), "god." He represents the demonic temptation to see oneself as divine and therefore better than others (i.e. the insidious idea that I am more enlightened, further along the Path, than you). The truth is that all men are inherently divine.

10. The pyramid formed from the square here is as follows:

Triangle No. 1 = Fire, red
Triangle No. 2 = Air, yellow
Triangle No. 3 = Fire, red
Triangle No. 4 = Fire, red

11. The presiding Egyptian deity of this square (three triangles of Fire and one of Air on the pyramid) is the beautiful and alluring goddess, Nephthys. Her name means "the Lady of the House" and her chief function is the dispersion of aggragates. She usually wears a low-cut gauze-like robe which is easily seen through and is very sensual. She can reduce any form into its formless essence by her penetrating gaze. She is the complement of her sister, Isis. Her filmy gown is usually crimson and blue.

12. The Sphynx in this pyramid should be male and look like a large lion with a human head. It will have wings.

13. Prior to Spirit Vision, face East and recite the Sixth Call. This Call reminds the magician that the subquadrant Fire of Fire is an area which is "a torment to the wicked and a garland to the righteous." In other words, one's experience here will be highly karmic in nature.

14. In summary, the Servient Square "D" of ADRE is a region where the lower human nature is consumed in a purification by fire. The goddess Nephthys acts as the feminine complement of the King, EDLPRNAA, and she assists those natural fiery forces of this Watchtower to consume the karma of anyone who enters here. If properly prepared, a magician can return with much of the Great Work accomplished. If not properly prepared, he can retrurn with all sorts of karmic problems immediately manifesting themselves. During this spirit vision, the magician has the chance to meet with any or all of the Angels mentioned above, and to benefit from these encounters. BIZAZ can give one a better sense of communication, even telepathy. IZAZ can help one to identifiy with his inner spiritual essence rather than *only* as a human being, which is but a temporary manifestation of this essence. MADRE also helps one to see his divine self (*i.e.* the spiritual body in Table III). ADRE can help one to eliminate transient human qualities and incorporate permanent ones. However, one must beware of spiritual pride embodied in the demon MAD who haunts this square.

15. *A Warning:* The Servient Square "D" contains powerful forces which will expose one's unconscious karma, in an effort to consume it. That which is not consumed in the fires of this square will nevertheless be exposed. For this reason they will surely manifest for good or ill upon one's return. *The student is thus warned not to meddle with this square until fully prepared.* One important preparation in any spirit vision like this is to map out the signposts such as this one beforehand. Sometimes the signposts show dangers and the square is best left until later. It cannot be overemphasized that large, shaggy, sharp-toothed monsters are not the prime danger in magic of this type. The danger is a psychological one,

and it is very real indeed. Things will happen to anyone who uses this magic, even if no Angels or deities are encountered at all. Just because a magician doesn't see a Demon, doesn't mean that the Demon isn't there. In the psychic world, thoughts are things. There is no such thing as *only* a thought or *merely* an impulse. If one enters "D" unprepared and then has terrible nightmares later, or comes down with the flu, or has an unfortunate accident, one is perfectly free to say "coincidence"; but one could also correctly say that this magic brought to fruition certain karmic seeds that lay unconscious, until the experience in "D" germinated them into manifestation.

HOW THE MAGIC WORKS:
AS ABOVE, SO BELOW

The Egyptian teaching "as above, so below" is the cornerstone of Western occultism and magic. It applies to Enochian Magic as well. The phrase means that one principle expresses itself on all of the cosmic planes and Aethyrs. For this reason, the Spiritual Plane can be understood by knowing the Physical Plane. Every universal principle in the physical world is also active in all thirty Aethyrs.

A corollary to the above rule is that man is a microcosm of the macrocosmic universe. Every universal principle in the world is also active in man. This idea expresses the general principle of correspondence upon which the art of magic is based. A correspondence exists between certain things in the universe. If this correspondence is known, then anything otherwise unknown can become known. For example, the invisible worlds, planes and Aethyrs that exist beyond the range of the physical senses, can become known through their correspondences. Furthermore, because man has a physical body which senses an objective physical world, it seems reasonable to propose that this principle holds equally well on all of these planes and Aethyrs. If so, then man has suitable vehicles on each cosmic plane with appropriate sensing organs to experience those planes. The truth of this proposition is demonstrated by dreams, because a dreamer is by definition one who leaves the physical body and functions on the Astral Plane in an astral body. The fact that most people are unconscious of what they are doing in dreams does not disprove the proposition. Rather it shows the frailty of human consciousness on the Astral Plane and the importance of magical exercises if one is to retain conscious control of himself and his surroundings.

Insofar as Enochian Magic is concerned, the Watch-towers and Aethyrs pertain both to the universe and to man. In a very real sense they are regions of the subtle worlds which surround and sustain the Earth. In another sense, equally valid, they are regions of the mind; psychological dimensions whose inhabitants are personifications of powerful psychic forces and impulses both unique and shared (i.e. residents of the personal and collective unconscious defined by Carl Jung). Hinduism likens man to waves that rise up on the surface of an ocean. As a wave, each person is discrete. But as all waves rise up from a common sea, so the consciousness of man rises up from a common subconsciousness. For this reason when any two magicians enter an Aethyr they will share certain experiences and not share others. These "shared experiences" are called *signposts*. Each Watchtower Square and Aethyr has its own signposts. Every magician should encounter these. They serve as buoys, or road signs, by marking safe passageways for those who travel in the Spirit Vision.

THE AETHYRS

The Governors of the Aethyrs: How to Obtain
Their Names

Each of the Aethyrs is presided over by at least three Governors. Their names are contained in the Watchtowers, 22 in each Tablet and three in the Black Cross. Figure 27 shows the sigils for these Governors and how their names are obtained. Each sigil has an arrow at the beginning of the name to show the proper direction of the letters.

There is a total of 92 Governors. This is an important magical number, being numerically equivalent to the Enochian word TOANT which means "love."

A careful count of 22 names from each Tablet and three from the Black Cross results in one missing name. An examination of Figure 27 will show that eight squares are not used for the sigils. In these eight squares, Dee had written the Enochian letters backwards. Presumably this was owing to the danger of seeing, or pronouncing, them even by accident. These letters are O and A from Air, L and (Y, L, N, H) from Water, A and (R, O) from Earth, and A and (O, P) from Fire: a total of thirteen letters and eight squares.

Crowley gives the missing secret name as PARAOAN and relates it to the 22nd Aethyr, LIN. The remaining backward letter is L and this is prefixed to one of the three names from the Black Cross thus forming the name LEXARPH (all three of these names are attributed to the 10th Aethyr, ZAX).

Two Aethyrs are given four Governors: the 30th, TEX, and the 22nd, LIN. The remaining 28 Aethyrs each have three.

The Call of the Thirty Aethyrs.

There is only one Call for all thirty Aethyrs. The name of any desired Aethyr is inserted into the blank space at the

Figure 27. The Sigils for the Governors of the Thirty Aethyrs.

beginning of the Call. The following Call should be recited prior to traveling in the Spirit Vision to any of the Aethyrs (Crowley's version is contained in Appendix B for comparison):

The Heavens that are in the (first, second, etc) Aethyr, (LIL, ARN, etc.) are mighty in those regions of the universe, and they carry out the Judgment of the Highest. To them it is said: Behold, the Face of your God, the beginning of Comfort, whose eyes are the brightness of the Heavens. He enables you to govern the Earth, and her unspeakable variety and furnishes you with the Power of Understanding so that you can carry out all things according to the Providence of Him who sits upon the Holy Throne, and who rose up in the Beginning, saying: The Earth, let her be governed by her parts, and let there be division in her, so that her glory may be both an eternal ecstasy and an inherent vexation.

Her course, let it run with the Heavens, and let her serve them like a handmaiden.

One season, let it mix with another, and let there be no creature upon her or within her that remains the same.

All of her members, let them have different qualities, and let no one creature be equal to another.

The creatures of reason who are on the Earth, such as man, let them disturb and eliminate one another; and their dwelling places, let their Names be forgotten.

The egotistical works of man, let them be destroyed.

His buildings, let them become caves for the beasts of the field.

Dim her understanding with darkness. Why? Because I am sorry that I have made Man. The Earth is well known for awhile, and for another while, she is a stranger, because she is the bed of a harlot, and the dwelling place of him who is fallen.

O Heavens, arise! The Lower Heavens are beneath you. Let them serve you! Govern those who govern! Cast down those who are likely to fall. Bring forth with those who increase, and destroy those who are rotten. Let no place remain in one number. Add and subtract until the stars are numbered.

Arise! Move! Appear before the Covenant of His Mouth which He has sworn to us in His Justice. Unveil the mysteries of your creation, and make us to be partakers of THE UNDEFILED KNOWLEDGE (IADNAMAD).

THE THIRTIETH AETHYR: TEX

Name: TEX is pronounced *Teh-etz* and means "The Aethyr that is in four parts."

Gematria: TEX = 419 = LONKHO (the fallen)
419 is also the Hebrew word TITh (serpent)
TEX = 413 = 59 x 7 where 59 = BALTOH
(the righteous)

Governors:

1. TA^{A}o^O$_A$G^{B}A   Tablet: Water   Sigil:
   a. Name: TAOAGLA,   Tah-oh-ah-geh-lah
   TA-NOAG-LA can mean "He who becomes the foremost."
   b. Gematria: TAOAGLA=73=ATH-ZEN
   (works of sacrifice)
   TAOAGLA=67=L-BALTOH
   (most righteous)

2. GEMNIMB   Tablet: Water   Sigil:
   a. Name: GENIMB,   Gem-nee-em-bah
   GEM-NIMB can mean "He who is only for a season"
   b. Gematria: GEMNIMB=313=HOLQ-PANPIR
   (to increase measurements)
   also 313=EOLIS BALZIZRAS
   (to make judgments)

3. AD^U$_V$ORPT   Tablet: Water   Sigil:
   a. Name: ADUORPT,   Ah-du-oh-rah-peh-teh
   A-DUORPT can mean "He who silently watches"
   b. Gematria: ADUORPT=228=QURLST
   (woman, handmaiden)

228 is also the Hebrew word IRChI
(lunar)
ADUORPT = 222, PRDZAR
(to deceive)

4. DO^X_ZM$_I$^{A}NU^I$_A$L   Tablet: Water   Sigil: $\curlyvee$

a. Name: DOZIAAL,   Doh-zodee-ah-ah-leh
DOZI-AAL can mean "He who estab-
lishes the night."

b. Gematria: DOZIAAL = 123 = MOZ (joy) =
LONDOH (kingdom)
123 is also the Hebrew word ONG
(pleasure, delight)
DOZIALL = 117 = NANBA (thorns) =
ZIZOP (vessel)
117 is also the Hebrew word OLIZ
(joyful)

Location: TEX is the lowest and most material of the
Aethyrs. It is located on the Etheric Plane, or Lower
Astral Plane which surrounds the Earth and is, in fact,
the etheric body of the Earth.

Brief Description: This Aethyr, as its name implies, is
divided into four major sections as follows:

North; the region of Karma and strong karmic forces.

East; the region of Desire and charged with all manner
of personal desires.

South; the region of Silence and a strong tendency
toward nonverbal communication because of
the difficulty in finding adequate words.

West; the region of personal limitation and a tendency
of the ego to realize its shortcomings.

Comment: TEX gives one a brief glimpse into the subtle
planes that exist immediately behind (or beyond) the
physical. The four fundamental occult teachings of

karma (limitations of action), desire (limitations of emotions), silence (limitations of language), and personal restriction (limitations of ego) are all found here. Hints of higher teachings are given, but as yet these seem only a promise yet unfulfilled.

THE TWENTY-NINTH AETHYR: RII

Name: RII is pronounced *Ree-ee* and means "The Aethyr of the mercy of heaven."

Gematria: RRI = 220 = OM MAD (knowledge of God)
also, 220 = 110x2, where 110 = LAMA
(a path)
and 220 = 22x10, where 22 = BALT (justice)
and 10 = ATH (works)

Governors:
1. VASTRIM   Tablet: Earth   Sigil:
   a. Name: VSTRIM   Vah-seh-tah-ree-em
   VAS-RIT-M can mean "He who is
   merciful."
   b. Gematria: VSTRIM = 342 = KAL BALT
   (solidification of justice)
   VASTRIM = 336 = LEVITHMONG
   (beasts of the field)
   336 is also the Hebrew word MKVOR
   (ugly)

2. ODRAXTI   Tablet: Earth   Sigil:
   a. Name: ODRAXTI   Oh-dar-ahtz-tee
   OD-RAX-TI can mean "He who opens
   up the east."
   b. Gematria: ORDAXTI = 609 = 203x3, where 203 =
   PIAMOL (righteousness)
   203 is also the Hebrew word BRA
   (created)
   and the Hebrew word ABR
   (destroyed)
   ODRAXTI   603   OXI-ZIN
   (mighty waters)

3. G^Mo^TMZIAM   Tablet: Earth   Sigil:

a.Name: GMOTZIAM   Geh-moh-teh-zodee-
ah-meh
G-OM-T-ZIAM can mean "He who
knows only himself."

b. Gematria: GMOTZIAM=302=151x2, where
151=ZORGE (love)
GMOTZIAM=296=148x2, where
148=ORSBA (intoxicated)
GMOTZIAM=290=RIOR (a widow)

Location: The 29th Aethyr is located on the Astral Plane.
This is the dream state, the plane of psychic fantasy, the
Heavens of the world's religions.

Brief Description: Like the 30th Aethyr, this too is divided
into four sections (there is a strong sense of direction
here):

South: This section is characterized by the realization
of the survival of consciousness after death; It is the
Kama-Loka of Theosophy, or at least a part of it.

East: This section is characterized by the desire for
revenge and for destruction of the wicked; there is a
strong sense of right and wrong.

West: This section is characterized by a sense of finality
and inevitability; evolution seems to be finished
here; strong sense of stagnation.

North: This section is characterized by judgment; karmic necessity; destiny; There is a feeling here that
karma is a huge wheel that rolls on and on forever.

Comment: RII gives one a clear look at what happens after
death for the average person. Life does, in fact, continue
on after death of the physical body. But the quality of
this life is of a restrictive nature. The religious person
enters heaven. The agnostic continues on in a dream-
like existence and may not even know that he has died.

The closed mind sees an end to all things. The open (but naive) mind sees the hopelessness of an endless cycle of births and deaths beyond his ability to control. The play between these dualistic viewpoints is strong here.

THE TWENTY-EIGHTH AETHYR: BAG

Name: BAG is pronounced *Bah-geh* and means "The Aethyr of doubt."

Gematria: BAG = 19 which is equal to the Hebrew word ChVH (to manifest)
also 19x2 = 38 = OL (to make)
and 19x3 = 57 = GOSAA (stranger)
57 is also the number for the Hebrew AVIM (terrible)

Governors:

1. ᵀ_LABNIXP   Tablet: Earth   Sigil: ꝯ
   a. Name: TABNIXP, Tah-ben-eetz-peh
   TABN-IXP can mean "He who governs"
   b. Gematria: TABNIXP = 539 = KORMEP
   (to number)
   TABNIXP = 533 = HOL-IOLKAM
   (to measure and bring forth)

2. ᴾ_FOKLSNI   Tablet: Earth   Sigil: 𝕌ᴧ
   a. Name: FOKLSNI, Foh-kel-ess-nee
   FO-KLZNI can mean "He who visits those in Heaven"
   b. Gematria: FOKLSNI = 458 = YOLKI (to bring forth)
   also 458 = 229x2, where 229 = SAANIR (parts, sections)

3. OXLOPAR   Tablet: Earth   Sigil: ꝟꝛ
   a. Name: OXOLPAR, Ohtz-loh-pər
   OXOL-PAR can mean "He who has them in his hands"
   b. Gematria: OXLOPAR = 583 = KOMMAH-IA
   (to bind up truth)

also 583=MIKA-IADNAH
(powerful knowledge)

Location: The 28th Aethyr is located in the Astral Plane in a subplane characterized by a strong sense of conscience, sin, and the need for purgative suffering.

Brief Description: A strong feeling of one's unworthiness pervades this Aethyr. Sin, especially karmic sin, is seen here as self-limiting. There is suffering here in a purgatory sense, and one feels that sorrow itself is a necessary factor to encounter if one is to spiritually progress. This Aethyr is filled with the symbols of dualism and one may feel that evil is as real and necessary as good. It is the inherent discriminating nature of the human mind that brings about this strong sense of dualism. If the magician looks carefully, he will detect a hint of the illusive nature of the ego here.

Comment: The power of restriction and doubt in this Aethyr comes from one's own sense of guilt and unworthiness, and thus from one's own karma. BAG is the result of one's identification with the human ego, which is seen as little better than an animal and, at best, a sinner. This kind of identification places a restriction on consciousness and prevents further progress. As long as one identifies himself as a human sinner, he will not be able to rise above BAG. The notion that man is more than an animal, that man can cast off egotistical impulses and desires and can retain a spiritual and purified nature, is considered a blasphemy by some, but is essential for the magician to rise into the higher Aethyrs.

THE TWENTY-SEVENTH AETHYR: ZAA

Name: ZAA is pronunced *Zodah-ah* and means "The
            Aethyr of solitude."
Gematria: ZAA=21=APA (that which is unchanging)
            21 is also equal to the Hebrew word AHIH
                    (existence)
            ZAA=15=GAH (spirit)=AP (unchanging)

Governors:
1. SAZIAMI   Tablet: Earth   Sigil: ⤙ᶴ
   a. Name: SAZIAMI,   Sah-zodee-ah-mee
               SA-Z-IA-MI can mean "He who has
                   true power"
   b. Gematria: SAZIAMI=238=VIRG (nests, home)
                   also 238=119x2, where 119=RAAS
                   (east)=ZIN (waters)
               SAZIAMI=232=MAZPRGE
                   (appearance of fire)

2. MATHVLA   Tablet: Earth   Sigil: ᗐⵍ
   a. Name: MATHVLA,   Mah-teh-hev-lah
               M-ATH-VLA can mean "He who ends
                   actions"
   b. Gematria: MATHVLA=190=VONPHO (wrath)
                   190 is also equal to the Hebrew word
                       QTz (the end)
               MATHVLA=184=DOSIG-IPA
                   (night of voidness)

3. ᴷoRPANIB   Tablet: Earth   Sigil: ᒧ ⌐
   a. Name: KORPANIB,   Koh-ar-pah-nee-beh
               KAR-PON-BI can mean "He who de-
                   stroys speech"

b. Gematria: KORPANIB=560=KOMOIN
(window to the void)
also 560=280x2, where 2803
VOVIN (dragon)
and 560 is equal to the Hebrew
ThNINIM (dragons)

Location: The 27th Aethyr is located at the apex of the Astral Plane where the primary characteristic is loneliness.

Brief Description: This Aethyr emphasizes man's basic nature of solitude. One is alone in the womb before birth, and returns to this aloneness after death. Because man has an individual or monadic essence, he is forever alone with himself and his reality. This Aethyr contains the feeling of separateness, of being an isolated entity separate and distinct from all other entities. In ZAA the magician will encounter the Great Heresy of Mahayana Buddhism—the awesome and terrible isolation of individuality.

The primary angel in ZAA is the goddess Hecate, who weeps continually for the suffering of humanity. Her tears turn into pearls which she offers to all who enter here. The magician must accept these pearls; he must incorporate within himself the precious characteristic of compassion if he expects to rise above ZAA. This goddess can also be seen as the Egyptian Hathor whose name, Het-Her, means "the place above." Hathor is an expression of the goddess Nut who represents infinite space. It is this quality of Space that is emphasized in ZAA.

Comment: When the magician realizes that he is not a lowly sinner and, in fact, has the potential for spiritual things, he can rise above BAG into ZAA. But his self-image is still restricted and distorted. He still clings to his humanity. This makes him see aloneness as loneliness. If emotional reactions to stimulation are equated with life, then the lack of such reactions will probably be interpreted as death. Life takes on meaning in the interactions of one's self with other selves. In this sense, ZAA is death. Here life is seen as a game wherein all the players must accept clearly defined ground rules. But because this game inevitably ends in death for each player, the only meaningful goal becomes how well the game itself is played. In ZAA one is able to consider how well he has been playing. This builds and otherwise modifies his character traits in preparation for his return to the game. The aloneness of ZAA is therefore a necessary condition in order to assimilate life experiences.

THE TWENTY-SIXTH AETHYR: DES

Name: DES is pronounced in one syllable as *Dess* and means "The Aethyr that accepts that which is."

Gematria: DES=21=APA (that which is unchanging)= ZAA (27th Aethyr)

DES and ZAA share their nature through the number 21.

also, 21x16=336, where 16=ZAH (within)

336 is the Hebrew word ROIVN (thought)

Governors:

1. POPHAND   Tablet: Earth   Sigil: ⌐ ⌐

   a. Name: POPHAND,   Poh-peh-hah-en-deh

   POPH-AN-D can mean "He who is divided into three parts"

   b. Gematria: POPHAND=109=DOSIG (night)= ZAR (ways, paths)

   109 is also the Hebrew word OGVL (circle, sphere)

   and 109x2=218, the number for the Hebrew IRCh (moon)

2. NIGRANA   Tablet: Earth   Sigil: ⌐⌐

   a. Name: NIGRANA,   Nee-gar-ah-nah

   NI-GRAA-N can mean "He who governs the 28 days of the moon"

   b. Gematria: NIGRANA 280=VOVIN (dragon)= IOU-GRAA (soul of the moon)

   280 is also the Hebrew word RP (terror)

3. ᴸᴮAZᴴᴷᴵᴴᴸM   Tablet: Earth   Sigil: ⌐ Ω

   a. Name: BAZHIIM,   Bah-zod-hee-ee-meh

148

BAZHI-IM can mean "He who makes use of the day"

b. Gematria: BAZHIIM = 231 = T-PRDZAR
(to decrease in proportion)
231 is also for the Hebrew word DKVRA (male)
BAZHIIM = 225 = T-PRDZAR
(to decrease in proportion)
also 225 = RAAGIOSL (Great King of the Water Tablet)
and 225 = 15x15, where 15 = ZAA (27th Aethyr)

Location: The 26th Aethyr is located at the lowest level of the Mental Plane where logic and reason hold sway over intuition.

Brief Description: This Aethyr is the realm of logic and reason. But the intuitive conviction that logic and reason are unable to get at truth, and in fact distort and limit truth, is like an undercurrent running through the Aethyr of DES. The Angel who guides one through DES is dressed in black. DES is torn by great forces of duality which sweep through it. Good and evil, sin and salvation, illusion and reality, all demand attention here. The intellect is hard pressed to cope with these dual forces. It feels its own inadequacy and its lamentations are thunders which boom from one end of DES to the other. This inability of the intellect to cope with duality is demonstrated in Zen Buddhism by the *koan* which the student is given to meditate on until it is fully understood. The forces flowing through DES are like a koan. At the top of this Aethyr, coincident with the death of the intellect, the magician will have a brief vision of the beautiful goddess Nut, the Eternal Feminine, the Mother of All, Infinite Space, whose body is jeweled with stars.

Comment: The death of one's discriminative faculties marks the birth of a higher type of consciousness. This is the great secret of the Mental Plane, that consciousness can function without the human mind, and without words, and even without forms.

Any magician who can enter DES has already learned to see life as a game but, due to the intellect, it takes the game very seriously. Logic and reason have been exalted. Now the magician can go no higher until he can *go beyond* logic and reason. This requires some degree of intuitive insight.

DES is covered by intellectual fog. The intellect desperately clings to dualism and sees clearly its own death in the higher Aethyrs, and quite naturally feels threatened. It seeks a rational solution to the problem of dualism but cannot find it any more than the Zen student can *explain* his koan. In order to rise above DES, the magician must be willing to drop all logical arguments and to bring to an end all intellectual dissections.

THE TWENTY-FIFTH AETHYR: VTI

Name: VTI is pronounced *Veh-tee* and means "The Aethyr of change."

Gematria: VTI=139=SIBSI (Covenant)=TOR
(23rd Aethyr)
VTI=133=OVOF (to be magnified)
133 is also the value of the Hebrew HChHLPH
(change)

Governors:

1. MIRZIND   Tablet: Earth   Sigil:
   a. Name: MIRZIND,   Mee-rah-zodee-en-deh
   MIR-ZIN-D can mean "He who is from the Waters of Torment"
   b. Gematria: MIRZIND=373=TA-TELOKH
   (like death)
   MIRZIND=367=MOMAO-OHIO
   (crown of woe)
   367 is also the Hebrew words MMIN
   ZKR (masculine) and AIShVN (black)

2. OB^UvAORS   Tablet: Earth   Sigil:
   a. Name: OBVAORS,   Oh-beh-vah-oh-rah-seh
   OBVA-ORS can mean "He who is half darkness"
   b. Gematria: OBVAORS=248=PI-BLIAR
   (places of comfort)
   also 248=SIBSI-DOSIG (covenant with the night)
   and 248 is the Hebrew word RChM
   (womb)

3. RANGLAM   Tablet: Earth   Sigil: ⌐⌐

   a. Name: RANGLAM,   Rah-neh-geh-lah-meh
                   R-ANGLA-M can mean "He who governs
                   his thoughts"

   b. Gematria: RANGLAM = 268 = BRGDO-OHIO
                      (sleep of woe)
               also 268 = LRASD-MOLAP
                    (disposer of men)

Location: The 25th Aethyr is in the Lower Mental Plane in a subplane of change between the old logic and reason of the intellect and the new intuition. It is a natural continuation of the 26th Aethyr, DES. On the Qabalistic Tree of Life, VTI is just under Tiphareth.

Brief Description: This Aethyr at first appears to be volatile and destructive. But this is only because destruction is necessary for creation, just as one must first die in order to be reborn. The chief characteristic of VTI is spiritual pride. The intuition has won over the intellect and the magician is now in VTI. The magician, if not forewarned, will be quick to pat himself on the back and to boast of his attainments. The Guiding Angel of VTI may approach the magician and close his mouth for him.

Comment: The magician leaves DES and enters VTI as a natural continuation of intuition over intellect. However, here the poison of spiritual pride will hold one until this pride can be cast aside. One is very apt to feel himself to be one of the Great Adepts of mankind because of his successes. There is a feeling in VTI that there is nowhere else to go; that there are no "higher" Aethyrs. The desire to "rest on one's laurels" is strong here because VTI will often appear like a great plateau. In order to rise higher, the magician will have to learn how to truly travel about in these Aethyrs.

THE TWENTY-FOURTH AETHYR: NIA

Name: NIA is pronounced *En-ee-ah* and means "The Aethyr of traveling."

Gematria: NIA=116=POILP (to be divided)=MABZA
                   (a robe)
          116 is also for the Hebrew word IVNIM
                    (doves)

Governors:
1. OR$^A_K{}^N_A{}^K_{NM}$IR   Tablet: Earth   Sigil:
   a. Name: ORAKAMIR,   Oh-rah-kah-mee-ar
                ORAK-A-MIR can mean "He who is above and below"
   b. Gematria: ORAKAMIR=692=ZAMRAN
                ZAKARE (to come into movement)
                also 692=SALMAN KHIRLAN
                    (House of Joy)

2. KH$^{LA}_{BT}{}^S_A$LP^O_S Tablet: Earth   Sigil:
   a. Name: KHIASALPS,   Keh-hee-ah-sal-pess
                KHIA-SALPS can mean "He of wondrous joy"
   b. Gematria: KHIASALPS=404=ABRAMIG-MOZ
                    (preparation of joy)
                404 is also the Hebrew word ShQD
                    (to hasten)

3. SOAGEEL   Tablet: Earth   Sigil:
   a. Name: SOAGEEL,   Soh-ah-geh-el
                SO-A-GE-EL can mean "He who helps the most"
   b. Gematria: SOAGEEL=79=HOLQ (to measure)=
                PAID (always)

also 79 = ELU-BESZ
(primordial matter)
and 79 is also the Hebrew word
DOH (mind)

Location: The 24th Aethyr is the Aethyr of astral traveling both through space and through time. It is at the apex of the Lower Mental Plane.

Brief Description: NIA is the region of traveling in the mental body. This traveling can be spacial (along the plane) or vibrational (through the cosmic planes) or durational (through time). The Aethyr is thus a preparation for all of the other planes and Aethyrs, especially for the 15th Aethyr.

In order to travel astrally in a "body of light" one must die to the personality and physical body. Entering NIA is therefore similar to dying, except that here a psycho-magnetic link (called the silver cord) still connects the mind with the body. In death this attachment is severed. Because of the nature of this out-of-body traveling, one's personal fears, loves, hates and so forth, must be put aside or else they can interfere and cause dissociation, insanity, and possibly even death. These Aethyrs are not without their dangers.

The magician who can travel about in NIA will probably see an impassible roof gleaming like steel over the top of this region. This is a Ring-Pass-Not for the magician at this stage of his development.

Comment: NIA is somewhat like a summary version of the lower six Aethyrs (TEX through VTI) and it combines the best characteristics of each. But there is a new factor added here. This new quality is joy, which is a true spiritual characteristic. Joy is intensified as one goes higher into the Aethyrs. The sense of joy is essential for the Great Work. The magician in NIA learns that life is inherently joyous, that the game of life is fun to play.

The Ring-Pass-Not in NIA is the barrier between the Lower Mental Plane and the Upper Mental Plane. In order to pass this barrier, the magician must pass beyond his normal human mind.

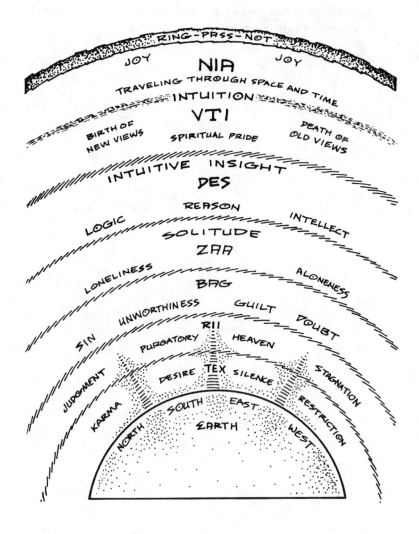

Figure 28. A Schematic Diagram of the Lowest Seven Aethyrs.

THE TWENTY-THIRD AETHYR: TOR

Name: TOR is pronounced *Toh-rah* and means "The
Aethyr that sustains [the universe]."

Gematria: TOR=139=SIBSI (covenant)=VTI (25th
Aethyr)
also 139x2=278, the Hebrew words GORH
(girl) and OVBR (fetus)
TOR=133=OVOF (to be magnified)
also 133x2=266, the Hebrew word MTzPVN
(conscience)

Governors:
1. RONOᴬₒMB   Tablet: Earth   Sigil: ⌐⌐
   a. Name: RONOAMB,   Roh-noh-ah-meh-beh
   RO-NOAMB can mean "He who protects the process of becoming"
   b. Gematria: RONOAMB=311=KAB (a rod)
   311 is also the value of the Hebrew
   words ShBT (a rod)
   and AISh (a man)

2. ONIZIMP   Tablet: Earth   Sigil: ⌐◁⌐
   a. Name: ONIZIMP,   Oh-nee-zodee-em-peh
   O-NIS-IMP- can mean "He who brings
   labor"
   b. Gematria: ONIZIMP=308=154x2, where 154=
   VAUL (to work)
   308 is also the Hebrew word BVQR
   (daybreak)
   ONIZIMP 302=151x2, where 151=
   ZORGE (love)
   302 is also the Hebrew word BQR
   (dawn)

3. ZAXANIN   Tablet: Earth   Sigil: ⌐

    a. Name: ZAXANIN,   Zod-ahtz-ah-nee-en
               Z-AX-ANIN can mean "He who names things."

    b. Gematria: ZAXANIN=581=KORMP-QAA
                     (to number creation)
                 also 581=KAL-YRPOIL
                 (to solidify what is divided)
               ZAXANIN=575=25x23 where 25=
               BESZ (matter);23=GAH-L
               (the highest spirit)

Location: The 23rd Aethyr is located on the Mental Plane in the region of the World Sustainer, the principle of causation. It is he who maintains and powers the Earth.

Brief Description: TOR contains the mystery of toil, and the virtue of labor. It contains the Cause for which the Earth is an effect. The universe is evolving, but not toward any fixed or permanent goal. The end of evolution is the beginning of involution and *vice versa*. The entire universe and everything in it, oscillates between states of potential and kinetic energy without conceivable end. Matter evolves from spirit and then involves back into it again. For this reason all labor is an on-going process of self-expression or self-unfoldment, called the Great Work. Man and the universe are effects of the labor of an infinite number of constituent parts, all working together. This idea is clearly seen in TOR.

Comment: The joy of traveling in NIA now gives way to the seriousness of labor in TOR. The energy needed to perpetuate the lower planes and Aethyrs is awesome. But, as Einstein showed, energy and matter are directly related and are interchangeable. In effect, the source of energy is infinite, and therefore the potential for creativity is infinite. There is a danger in TOR that the magician will lose the sense of joy acquired in NIA and take creative manifestation too seriously. He should remember that the chief difference between work and play is one's attitude.

THE TWENTY-SECOND AETHYR: LIN

Name: LIN is pronounced *El-ee-en* and means "The Aethyr of the void."

Gematria: LIN=118=GONO (faith)

              118 is also the value of the Hebrew ChLP (change, renewal)

Governors:

1. O^{s}zIDAIA   Tablet: Air   Sigil:

   a. Name: OZIDAIA,   Oh-zodee-dah-ee-ah

                AOZ-IAD-IA can mean "He who is the god of truth"

   b. Gematria: OZIDAIA=175=OIAD-NAZPS
                   (sword of justice)

                also 175x3=525=KHIRLAN (joy)

                OZIDAIA=169=RIT (mercy)

2. KALZIRG   Tablet: Earth   Sigil:

   a. Name: KALZIRG,   Kal-zodee-ar-geh

                KALZ-IRG can mean "He who is in the firmament"

   b. Gematria: KALZIRG=491=KOMSELHA-
                   TABGES (a circular recess)

                491 is also the Hebrew word PUThH
                   (vagina)

                KALZIRG=485=ILONON-
                 MONONS (branches of the heart)

                485 is also the Hebrew word ThDOH
                 (mind, consciousness)

3. LAZDIX^{R}ı   Tablet: Water   Sigil:

   a. Name: LAZDIXR,   Lah-zodee-tzar

                LAS-DIXR can mean "He who brings down a bounty."

b. Gematria: LAZDIXR=587=YOLKI-MOZ
                    (to bring forth joy)
               LAZDIXR=581=ESIASKH-
                    QUASAHI (brother of delight)

4. PARAOAN   Tablet: 7 of 8   Sigil:
                   backward letters from
                   all four Tablets

a. Name: PARAOAN,   Pah-rah-oh-ah-em
                   PAR-AOAN can mean "He who has
                   eyes"

b. Gematria: PARAOAN=207=NIISO (come away)
                   207 is also the Hebrew word AGRAB
                         (a scorpion)
                  also 207x2=414=KRAL
                      (joy, pleasure)

Location: The 22nd Aethyr is located at a position in the Archetypal Plane where the occult doctrine of polarities becomes self-evident. It marks the beginning of non-dualism, which intensifies as one rises higher. Because of this shift in viewpoint toward the mystical, LIN is an Aethyr of change and renewal.

Brief Description: Consciousness in this Aethyr is in the first stages of the mystical state called *samadhi,* wherein the human personality is cast aside. Here the beginning of form can be seen as the very sense of extension in space. In addition, the complement of form, the formless, can be seen directly as an endless Void which gives the Aethyr its name. Actually this void in LIN is only an appearance. It *seems* void to the human mind that experiences it. The higher Aethyrs are no more formless than the deep sleep state, although this often seems a void when waking.

Comment: The Aethyr of LIN is the region where form and the formless merge into each other. It represents a dramatic change in one's viewpoint. The magician who enters here must look with eyes other than the human, else he will see only desolation.

THE TWENTY-FIRST AETHYR: ASP

Name: ASP is pronounced *Ahs-peh* and means "The Aethyr of causation."

Gematria: ASP=22=BALT (justice)
22 is also the value of the Hebrew word TVBH (good)

Governors:

1. KHⁱₕRZPA   Tablet: Air   Sigil: ✔

   a. Name: KHLIRZPA,   Keh-helee-rah-zod-pah
   KHIRL-SAP can mean "He who enjoys loud sounds"

   b. Gematria: KHLIRZPA=493=KNILA-ZEN
   (blood sacrifice)
   KHLIRZPA=487=MOZ-TELOKH
   (joy of death)
   487 is also the Hebrew word
   ALIMUTh (violence)

2. TOANTOM   Tablet: Air   Sigil:

   a. Name: TOANTOM,   Toh-ah-en-toh-em
   TOANT-OM cn mean "He who loves knowledge"

   b. Gematria: TOANTOM=224=BAHAL-A-
   AMMA (He whose cry is cursed)
   224 is also the Hebrew DKR (male)
   TOANTOM=212=TORZU (to rise up)
   212 is also the Hebrew ChDR
   (to enclose)

3. VIXPAG   Tablet: Air   Sigil:

   a. Name: VIXPALG,   Veetz-pah-leh-geh
   V-IX-ALPG can mean "He who consumes."

163

b. Gematria: VIXPALG = 561 =
KNILA-ORS
(the blood of darkness)
also 561 = MALPRG-ZOKH
(the burning up of the past)

Location: The 21st Aethyr is a continuation of the previous Aethyr in the Archetypal Plane. Here one confronts the reflection of the spirit or *atma* of man.

Brief Description: ASP is the location of the reflection of *atma* below the Abyss. It provides a distorted vision of man's spiritual nature. Here existence itself appears as an annihilation. The entire region at first seems an abomination and horror. There is little joy here. In ASP the magician comes face to face with his own reincarnating ego. Here is that part of himself that does the reincarnating into the lower planes. The three Governors of ASP all work together to silence the illusion of the ego and for this reason will at first appear hideous monsters or Demons.

Comment: The sense of desolation in ASP is the continuation of the sense of loneliness first experienced in ZAA (the 27th Aethyr). It is due to an erroneous sense of identification. The magician still identifies himself with a single incarnated ego. Therefore the realms above him here appear black and ominous. His own past and future lives can be seen here so that a shift in his sense of identity is necessary in order to properly assimilate these experiences. Insanity is but one real possibility. The magician in ASP must shift his sense of identity from ego to Ego, from a single human being to a reincarnating Ego which has many human expressions.

THE TWENTIETH AETHYR: KHR

Name: KHR is pronounced *Keh-har* and means "The Aethyr of the wheel."

Gematria: KHR=401=KHIDAO (diamonds)=TOTO-NOR-MOLAP (cycles of the sons of men) 401 is also the value of the Hebrew word ATh (essence)

Governors:

1. ZILDRON   Tablet: Air   Sigil:

   a. Name: ZILDRON, Zodee-el-dar-oh-en ZILDR-ON can mean "He who sets in flight"

   b. Gematria: ZILDRON=261=ZAMRAN (to appear) 261 is also the Hebrew MChZVR (a cycle) ZILDRON=255=ZAMRAN (to appear) 255 is also the Hebrew MZRCh (East)

2. PARZIBA   Tablet: Air   Sigil:

   a. Name: PARZIBA, Par-zodee-bah PAR-SIB-A can mean "He who promises"

   b. Gematria: PARZIBA=195=ETHARZI (in peace) also 195=13x15, where 15 is the Hebrew ZCh (to force, impel) and 13 is the Hebrew HGH (wheel) PARZIBA=189=FISIS-QAA (to make a creation)

165

3. TOTOKAN   Tablet: Air   Sigil:

    a. Name: TOTOKAN,   Toh-toh-kan

                  TOTO-KAN can mean "He who drives
                  the cycles"

    b. Gematria: TOTOKAN=434=ZAKAREF
                  (visitor)

                  TOTOKAN=422=VNIG-MATORB
                  (the need for repetition)

Location: The 20th Aethyr is located in a subplane of the Mental Plane where the whole world appears as a huge rotating wheel. The occult doctrine of cycles is self-evident here.

Brief Description: The magician who enters KHR will see the whole world as a tremendous spinning wheel. He may even see the hand of He who spins it. He will also sense that there is little purpose to it all; the Being who spins the wheel does so for His own pleasure. A close inspection will reveal that this wheel is both seductive and deceptive. Its allure is due to the fun and pleasure that it promises. Its deceit is its demand to be taken seriously. It contains games such as politics and religion which all too often turn the promised pleasure into pain and sorrow.

Comment: The magician in KHR should be able to see both sides of the universe; the *mayavic* deceptions which perpetuate bondage and false identifications, and the joyous expressions of love and beauty in form and color. The universe can be seen either way because, in a sense, it is both simultaneously. The formlessness of ASP gives way to a higher sense of form in KHR. The wheel of the universe is seen with spiritual eyes and as such the magician can see the inside as clearly as the outside.

THE NINETEENTH AETHYR: POP

Name: POP is pronounced *Poh-peh* and means "The
Aethyr of division."

Gematria: POP=48=LOE (12th Aethyr)
and 48=24x2, where 24=LEA (16th Aethyr)
=PAZ (4th Aethyr)
also 48=ELO (first)=TALHO (cup)
48 is also the value of the Hebrew words
ChIL (a woman)
and KVKB (a star)

Governors:

1. TORZOXI   Tablet: Air   Sigil:
   a. Name: TORZOXI,   Toh-razod-oh-tzee
              TORZ-OXI can mean "He who rises
              up in strength"
   b. Gematria: TORZOXI=638=VOVIN-TELOKH
                  (Dragon of Death)
                  also 638=MIKA-ZILDARH
                  (mighty flier)
                  TORZOXI 632=316x2, where 316 is the
                  Hebrew AIShH (a woman)
                  TORZOXI 626=313x2, where 313=
                  GEMNIMB (Governor of TEX)

2. AB^RAIOND   Tablet: Air   Sigil:
   a. Name: ABRAIOND, Ah-bar-ahee-oh-en-deh
              ABRA-I-OND can mean "He who pre-
              pares his kingdom"
   b. Gematria: ABRAIOND=261=ZILDRON
                  (Governor of KHR)
                  also 261=ZAMRAN (to appear)
                  and 261 is the Hebrew DRAVN
                  (an abomination)

3. OMAGRAP   Tablet: Air   Sigil:

   a. Name: OMAGRAP,   Oh-mah-gar-ah-peh
                OM-GRAAP can mean "He of lunar
                knowledge"

   b. Gematria: OMAGRAP = 249 = SIATRIS
                    (a scorpion)
                249 is also the Hebrew MGVR
                    (fear, terror)

Location: The 19th Aethyr is also on the Mental Plane; in a region containing the Priestess of the Silver Star. This priestess is the goddess Isis and she is located on the Qabalistic Tree of Life on the path of *gimel.* This places POP just above Tiphareth.

Brief Description: POP is an Aethyr of initiation. Here the magician is initiated into the karmic need for violence, bloodshed and death; characteristic attributes of human development. The initial vision in POP often results in a alphabet of daggers wherein each dagger symbolizes the sharp penetrating power of thought. The dagger is also used as a glyph for a sunbeam or ray of light; light itself being a symbol for consciousness. These daggers seen in POP are therefore usually related to an alphabet to illustrate how thoughts go together to form communication systems. The actual Aethyr is difficult to enter. It contains conflicting forces and there is a feeling here that life itself is surrounded by violence and death. The magician will usually meet the Guiding Angel, the Priestess of the Silver Star. Her function is to initiate anyone who enters here into a higher sense of life and the meaning of life. She personifies the spiritual impulse in man and imbodies the spiritual current, and she offers this current to all who can enter POP.

Comment: The imagery of life surrounded by violence and death can take many forms. It symbolizes the idea that existence is a series of conflicts of some kind. Good fights evil, life fights against death, and so on. All progress must be earned. No Adept can give spiritual insight to another. However, they can give initiation if one is properly prepared and ready for it.

THE EIGHTEENTH AETHYR: ZEN

Name: ZEN is pronounced *Zod-en* and means "The Aethyr of Sacrifice."

Gematria: ZEN=69=GOHO (to speak)=IP (not)
             69 is also the value of the Hebrew words
                  IGVN (desolation)
             and ABVS (an enclosure)
       ZEN=21x3, where 21=ZAA (27th Aethyr)
        also 63x2=126=OMA (understanding)

Governors:

1. NABAOMI   Tablet: Air   Sigil:

   a. Name: NABAOMI,   Nah-bah-oh-mee
                  NABA-OMI can mean "He who knows pain"

   Gematria: NABAOMI=247=IADNAH-GRAA
                  (knowledge of the moon)

2. ZAFASAI   Tablet: Air   Siblet:

   a. Name: ZAFASAI,   Zodah-fah-sahee
                  Z-AFA-SA-I can mean "He who is in emptiness"

   b. Gematria: ZAFASAI=97=HOLQ-AFFA
                  (measurement of emptiness)
              97 is also the Hebrew word AMUN
                  (changeless)
             ZAFASAI=91=TABAAN-AP
                  (unchanging governor)
             also 91=13x7, where 13 is the Hebrew
                word BHV (emptiness)

3. ᵛvA⅃PAMB   Tablet: Air   Sigil:

   a. Name: VALPAMB,   Val-pah-meh-beh

VAL-PAMB can mean "He who is the beginning and the end"

b. Gematria: VALPAMB = 194 = BITOM (fire) = EMETGIS (seal) = PARADIZ (virgin) also 194 = 97x2, where 97 = ZAFASAI (Governor no. 2 above)

Location: The 18th Aethyr is located on the Mental Plane at the place of an important initiation—the initiation of the crucifixion.

Brief Description: One who can enter ZEN will learn the esoteric meaning of sacrifice and crucifixion. First, one must be free of all personal desires, thoughts, regrets and attachments. This is an essential preparation for safe passage through this Aethyr. The main vision encountered is some type of a crucifixion. One possibility here is the Egyptian ritual of the King's Chamber in the Great Pyramid of Gizah. There a candidate was made to lay in the lidless sarcophagus for three days and nights while his subtle body roamed the planes and Aethyrs. If successful, he reached the 8th Aethyr and obtained a direct awareness of his own inner divinity. In other words, he became initiated, and was considered an Adept. In ZEN, one will see two types of crucifixion. In one, the higher Self is crucified on the cross of matter. This idea is symbolized in the Tarot by the Hanged Man. In the second form, the lower self is crucified in a tomb (or womb) of darkness in order to free consciousness. One is a descent into matter, the other is an ascent into spirit.

Comment: In ZEN the magician will see that birth and death are two forms of crucifixion. Both illustrate the principle of sacrifice, and in both the real sacrifice made is the break in the continuity of consciousness. Only an Adept can travel through all of the Aethyrs and retain continuity of consciousness (and therefore memory). The magician who can enter ZEN will learn how to maintain a continuity of consciousness. He will then be able to undergo crucifixion without sacrifice.

THE SEVENTEENTH AETHYR: TAN

Name: TAN is pronounced *Tah-en,* and means "The
Aethyr of one's equilibrium."

Gematria: TAN=65=BI (voice)
also 65x2=130=SOBOLN (West)
130 is also the Hebrew word HPLIH
(discrimination)
TAN=59=BALTOH (the righteous)
also 59x2=118=LIN (22nd Aethyr)
and 59x7=413=TEX (30th Aethyr)

Governors:
1. SIGMORF Tablet:Air Sigil:
   a. Name: SIGMORF, See-geh-moh-rah-feh
SIG-MOR-F can mean "He who visits
the darkness"
   b. Gematria: SIGMORF=298=BALZIZRAS-OIAD
(judgment of the just)
298 is also the Hebrew RChMIM
(mercy)

2. A\u1D42uDROPT Tablet: Air Sigil:
   a. Name: AYDROPT, Ah-yeh-deh-roh-peh-teh
AY-DROP-T can mean "He who sees
us with equality"
   b. Gematria: AYDROPT=218=TORZU (to rise up)
218 is also the Hebrew word IRCh
(moon)
AYDROPT=212=TORZU (to rise up)
=TOANTOM (Governor of 21st
Aethyr)
212 is also the Hebrew word ZRH
(harlot)

3. TOKARZI   Tablet: Air   Sigil:

a. Name: TOKARZI,   Toh-kar-zodee
               T-O-KARZI can mean "He of such
               equality"

b. Gematria: TOKARZI=514=VOVIN-MATORB
               (Dragon of Repetition)
               TOKARZI=508=127x4, where 127=
               IADNAH (knowledge)
               508 is also the Hebrew ShChR
               (dawn)

Location: The 17th Aethyr is the region of the Mental Plane
that contains the Karmic Balance. This balance produces
cyclic changes throughout the universe from its continuous efforts to reach equilibrium.

Brief Description: The initial vision here is usually of the
Guiding Angel who explains that all reality is relative.
Things are real only in relation to the consciousness
that experiences them. The magician will then be shown
the Balance of TAN which is, of course, karmic. This
karmic balance strives to bring the universe to an
equilibrium which would quite naturally destroy the
universe as we know it. However, the Balance con-
siders all imbalance as evil and seeks to equalize it.
Actually karma itself can be considered to be the result
of this huge Balance of TAN.

Comment: The symbol of the balance illustrates that karma
seeks an equilibrium for the forces of duality which
define the universe. Karma and duality are dependent
principles, neither of which could exist without the
other. The entire idea of morality and ethics must be
faced in TAN, where good and evil, right and wrong, are
weighed in the karmic balance of the universe.

THE SIXTEENTH AETHYR: LEA

Name: EA is pronounced *Eleh-ah* and means "The first Aether of the [higher] Self."

Gematria: LEA=24=TAPA (poison)=PAZ (4th Aethyr)
also 24x2=48=LOE (12th Aethyr)=POP (19th Aethyr)
and 24 is the value of the Hebrew GVIH (body)

Governors:

1. K^{U}v K^{U}A RPT   Tablet: Air   Sigil:

    a. Name: KUKUARPT,   Ku-ku-rah-peh-teh
KUKU-ARP-T can mean "He who replaces what was before with something similar"

    b. Gematria: KUKUARPT=864=54x16, where 54=
TALHO (cup)
and 16=TA (likeness)
864 is also the Hebrew words AShTH ZNVNIM (women of whoredom)
KUKUARPT=858=OADO-KIKLE-BABALON (to weave the mysteries of Babalon)
also 858=143x6, where 143=
MOLAP (MANKIND)

2. LAUAKON   Tablet: Air   sigil:

    a. Name: LAUAKON,   Lah-u-ah-koh-en
A-ULAKON can mean "The happy one"

    b. Gematria: LAUAKON=470=ZAMRAN-BLIORA (appearance of comfort)
470 is also the Hebrew word OTh (time)

3. SOKHIAL Tablet: Air Sigil:
 a. Name: SOKHIAL, Soh-keh-hee-al
      SOKH-IAL can mean "He who burns
      up the past"
 b. Gematria: SOKHIAL=412=MALPRG-IALPRG
      (burning fiery flames)
      412 is also the Hebrew ChDTh
      (new)
Primary Angel of this Aethyr: BABALON
 a. Name: BABALON is pronounced *Bah-bah-*
      loh-en and means "wicked" or "evil."
 b. Gematria: BABALON=110=TOANTA (lust)
Location: The 16th Aethyr is located on the Mental Plane in
a region of change and transition. Here one begins to
identify himself as a spiritual being.

Brief Description: The Guiding Angel of this Aethyr is
named Babalon. She is extremely alluring and enticing.
If the magician who enters here were to imagine the
most beautiful woman in the universe (an obviously
relative concept), such would be his vision of the angel
here. In the duality of objectivity and subjectivity,
Babalon personifies objectivity and the beast upon
which she often rides symbolizes subjectivity. The
magician in LEA feels that his consciousness is like an
unruly beast in need of discipline. It is driven willy-nilly
about the Aethyr by the seductive nature of the environment. Because the enchanting beauty of LEA is
available to all who enter here, she is sometimes fig-
uratively called a harlot (the Enochian word
BABALOND means "harlot").

 A second Angel will then approach the magician.
He personifies the past, especially the personal past
(and therefore karma) of the magician. He will lament
bitterly because he knows that he is dying. If asked, he

can show a vision of the Tarot trump of the Lightning Struck Tower, the 27th path of the Tree of Life. He will also provide a vision of one's spiritual self, but at this level of understanding it usually appears irrational and quite mad. For this reason it is called a *beast*. The Angel knows quite well that this beast will someday slay him. He may show this in a vision to the magician. One may even glimpse the ultimate victory of this beast, the spiritual self.

Comment: In LEA the great duality of the subjective self and the objective world is seen symbolically. This vision generally (but not always) takes the form of a beautiful naked woman riding upon an unruly beast of some sort. The attraction between these two polarities of Babalon and the beast is called *lust*. This lust is the theme of the Tarot card that symbolizes the 9th path of the Tree of Life, which connects the Sephiroths, Chesed and Geburah.

THE FIFTEENTH AETHYR: OXO

Name: OXO is pronounced *Oh-tzoh* and means "The
Aethyr of dancing."

Gematria: OXO=460=GLO-KRAL (things of joy)
460 is also the value of the Hebrew NShIQ
(to kiss, to come together)
also 460=230x2, where 230=ROR (the sun)
230 is also the Hebrew word KDVR
(the Earth)

Governors:

1. TAHA^N_MDO   Tablet: Air   Sigil:
   a. Name: TAHAMDO,   Tah-hah-meh-doh
   TA-HAM-DO can mean "He who lives
   according to his name"
   b. Gematria: TAHAMDO=146=IAOD-GLO
   (beginning of things)
   TAHAMDO=140=TIANTA (a bed)

2. NO^T_KIABI   Tablet: Air   Sigil:
   a. Name: NOKIABI,   Noh-kee-ah-bee
   NOK-IA-BE can mean "Servant who
   speaks the truth"
   b. Gematria: NOKIABI=511=NOKO-LONSA
   (the servant of everyone)

3. TASTO^Z_XO   Tablet: Air   Sigil:
   a. Name: TASTOXO,   Tah-seh-toh-tzoh
   TAST-OXO can mean "He who initiates dancing"
   b. Gematria: TASTOXO=491=OXO-BESZ
   (dancing matter)=KALZIRG
   (Governor of 22nd Aethyr)

491 is also the Hebrew word PUThH
(vagina)
TASTOXO = 479 = BI-KRAL
(voice of joy)

Location: The 15th Aethyr is on a subplane of the Mental Plane where all life is seen directly as a great dance. This is the play of Brahman taught in Hinduism.

Brief Description: The vision of OXO is based on the realization that life needs no purpose or goal other than itself. The purpose of life is to live. When one enters OXO, he will usually see a beautiful goddess dancing. Some say that this is the biblical Salome where, by gematria, SALOME = 151 = ZORGE (love) = HOATH BABA-LON (a true worshipper of Babalon). Whatever the case, she is indeed a reflex of the seductive world personified by Babalon. She is also a form of that aspect of the Hindu Brahman which is called *ananda* or bliss (Brahman is often called *sat-sit-ananda* or existence-consciousness-bliss). Her dance expresses the ecstatic joy of spiritual consciousness. It is a visual representation of the highly occult "music of the spheres." If a magician looks closely, he will usually see a rose here in one form or another. The feminine symbol of the rose is an apt glyph for the atmosphere of OXO.

Comment: OXO contains the sense of joy that began in NIA (24th Aethyr). Here the joy that was found in the harmony of the Aethyrs is intensified. Life is now seen as a divine dance, the *lila* of Hinduism. From the viewpoint of the serious and time-oriented ego, OXO appears as a terrible blasphemy. The message of OXO is that the creativity of divinity causes matter to flow from spirit until an equilibrium point is reached and then causes this matter to return back into its spiritual essence. This endless cyclic flow of the universe is seen as a joyous game in OXO.

THE FOURTEENTH AETHYR: VTA

Name: VTA is pronounced *Veh-tah* and means "The Aethyr of semblances."

Gematria: VTA=85=VLS (the outermost, the most distant)

85 is also the value of the Hebrew word MILH (circumcision)

VTA=79=HOLQ (measured)

79 is also the value of the Hebrew word GUO (to die)

Governors:

1. TE^K_DOAND   Tablet: Fire: Sigil:

  a. Name: TEDOAND,   Teh-doh-ah-en-deh

T-ED-ADNO can mean "He who demands obedience"

  b. Gematria: TEDOAND=113=ZIN (waters)

113 is also the Hebrew PLG (a stream, brook)

TEDOAND=107=HOATH-ADNA (one who worships obedience)

2. VI^U_VIPOS   Tablet: Fire   Sigil:

  a. Name: VIVIPOS,   Vee-vee-poh-seh

VIV-POSI can mean "He of many repetitions"

  b. Gematria: VIVIPOS=306=MATORB-TOTO-A (one who repeats)

306 is also the Hebrew AShH (a woman)

3. ^V_OOANA^M_NB   Tablet: Fire   Sigil:

  a. Name: VOANAMB,   Voh-ah-nah-em-beh

VAOAN-MB can mean "He to whom truth is relative"

  b. Gematria: VOANAMB=257=MONONS

180

(the heart)
257 is also the Hebrew ChRTM
(a magician)
and MRIBH (discord)

Location: The 14th Aethyr is on the Mental Plane in a region that contains the City of the Pyramids. This region partakes of both the darkness of Daath and the severity of Geburah on the Tree of Life, and is probably somewhere along the 7th path, the Lovers of the Tarot.

Brief Description: VTA is the home of those Adepts who have left the world of form and now reside in a formless darkness. They will appear black and lifeless to the magician who can enter here because they are without emotions of any kind. Their home is called the City of the Pyramids and it is covered with the thick black smoke of solemnity. The Aethyr is pervaded with a current of transiency. The transient nature of all things is felt here as a living presence and is sometimes called the "Great One of the Night of Time." Everyone who enters here will encounter him in one form or another. In the inky blackness of VTA countless Masters sit very still and quiet, looking like dark pyramids. They can neither see nor hear nor speak. The have eliminated all personal desire and lust for life.

Comment: The pyramid is both a place of initiation and a tomb. The Masters of VTA combine both of these possibilities. They are both initiated and dead. They represent those people who have used yoga or magic for personal gain. They have burnt-out desire and have risen to this lofty spiritual height. But to what end? They represent the lowest form of Pratyeka-Buddha. This is an Adept who seeks only his own salvation. Only by being like the bodhisattva who has compassion for others, can one hope to ascend the Aethyrs all the way to LIL, the first.

THE THIRTEENTH AETHYR: ZIM

Name: ZIM is pronounced *Zodee-mah* and means "The Aethyr of application (or practice)."

Gematria: ZIM=159=TABAAN-FIFALZ
(governor who weeds out)
also 159=53x3, where 53=BALTOH
(righteous)
53 is also the Hebrew word GN (a garden)
ZIM=153=LORSL (flowers)=ABRAASSA-ATH (to provide work)

Governors:

1. GEKAOND   Tablet: Fire   Sigil:
   a. Name: GEKAOND,   Geh-kah-oh-en-deh
               GE-K-ADNO can mean "He who only obeys"
   b. Gematria: GEKAOND=408=QURLST-NEMO
               (Nemo's handmaiden)
               also 408=204x2, where 204=PAPNOR (remembrance)

2. LAPARIN   Tablet: Fire   Sigil:
   a. Name: LAPARIN,   Lah-pah-ree-en
               LAP-AR-IN can mean "He who is the protector of man"
   b. Gematria: LAPARIN=239=FIFALZ-GROSB
               (weeding out the unworthy)
               239 is also the Hebrew word GURL (fate)

3. DOKEPAX   Tablet: Fire   Sigil:
   a. Name: DOKEPAX,   Doh-keh-pahtz
               DO-KEP-AX can mean "He who names only great names"
   b. Gematria: DOKEPAX=759=KORMP-ROR

(to number the sun)
and 759=23x33, where 23 is the
Hebrew ChDUH (joy)
and 33 is the Hebrew ABL (sorrow)

Primary Angel of this Aethyr: NEMO

A. Name: NEMO can be pronounced either *Neh-moh* in two syllables or *En-em-oh* in three syllables. The name means "Master of the Temple" and refers to an initiatory title. This name spelled backwards is OM-EN which means "know thyself."

b. Gematria: NEMO=180=LIMLAL (treasure) = MAD-NETAAB (divine government)

Location: The 13th Aethyr is on the Mental Plane at the sub-plane of Nemo, the Silent Watcher of mankind.

Brief Description: ZIM is the Aethyr of NEMO, the Master of the Temple of Great White Brotherhood. This is a universal organization of men and women whose sole task is to help others to realize their spiritual potential. It is this organization which keeps the spirit of love and brotherhood alive in the world. One of the leaders of this group is called Nemo and he resides in the 13th Aethyr. The magician who enters ZIM will usually see Nemo tending his enormous garden like a devoted horticulturist. The garden symbolizes the universe. The flowers that occasionally can be seen to spring up from this garden are the new members of the organization, sometimes called the Hierarchy of Compassion.

Comment: The vision of Nemo in ZIM emphasizes the importance of compassion and concern for others. Without compassion, one will probably become a pyramid-like Adept in VTA. Nemo represents a principle form of this compassion; the desire to help others no matter how long it takes and with no thought for any personal reward.

THE TWELFTH AETHYR: LOE

Name: LOE is pronounced *El-oh-eh* and means "The
            first Aethyr of glory."

Gematria: LOE=48=POP (19th Aethyr)=TALHO
                        (a cup)
                48 is also the value of the Hebrew ChIL
                        (a woman)
                also 48=6x8, where 6=A (I, self), and 8=G
                        (not, void)

Governors:

1. TAPAMAL   Tablet: Fire   Sigil:
   a. Name: TAPAMAL,   Tah-pah-mal
                TA-PAM-AL can mean "He who is
                like he was at the beginning"
   b. Gematria: TAPAMAL=134=TAFA-BABALON
                        (poison of BABALON)
                also 134=ED-NAS-GOSAA
                        (receiver of strangers)
                TAPAMAL=128=TIANTA (a bed)
                128 is also the Hebrew HChLPH
                        (change)

2. GEDOONS   Tablet: Fire   Sigil:
   a. Name: GEDOONS,   Geh-doh-oh-ness
                GE-DO-ONS can mean "He who elimin-
                ates your name"
   b. Gematria: GEDOONS=139=SIBSI (covenant)
                        =TOR (23rd Aethyr)
                also 139=FIFALZ-DODSEH
                        (elimination of vexation)

3. AM^BvRIOL   Tablet: Fire   Sigil:
   a. Name: AMBRIOL,   Ah-em-beh-ree-oh-leh

AM-BLIOR can mean "He who con-
tinuously comforts"
b. Gematria: AMBRIOL=299=ZUMVI (seas)=
BLIAR-GRAA (comfort of the moon)
299 is also the Hebrew word
AVRHLBNH (moonlight)

Location: The 12th Aethyr is located on the Mental
Plane at the place of the Mystery of Babalon.

Brief Description: LOE contains the leaders of the Hierarchy of Compassion, those who have given their life's
blood for others. It also contains the fate of the so-called
Black Brothers, those who seek to avoid the Abyss
because of fear or egoism. Those who are able to rise
above VTA but lack compassion congregate here. The
magician who enters LOE can see the chariot which is
the symbol of the 8th path of the Tree of Life. This path
crosses the Abyss while connecting the Sephiroths
Geburah and Binah. There the Mystery of Babalon will
be seen. This mystery was first sighted in LEA (16th
Aethyr) and is intensified here. Babalon will again be
seen riding a beast. Here the beast will have the title
"Lord of the City of Pyramids" and it is the inner divinity
of the magician, but more self-conscious than before.

Comment: LOE is the natural culmination of compassion
which is developed over the preceding Aethyrs. In LOE
one has to shed the last taint of a personal ego. Here the
magician will feel that compassion for others is a sacred
duty, a holy trust. However, there usually remains a
tiny subtle thought that says something like, "Look at
me, I am an Adept. I am working for your benefit.
Therefore you should give me your gratitude and respect." Even this kind of thought, an expression of
spiritual selfishness, must be eliminated.

THE ELEVENTH AETHYR: IKH

Name: IKH is pronounced *Ee-keh* and means "The Aethyr of tension."

Gematria; IKH=361=KAL-TOL (solidification of everything)

and 361=19x19, where 19 is the Hebrew word ChVH (to manifest)

and 19=BAG (3rd Aethyr)

361 is also the Hebrew word AShIN (foundation)

Governors:

1. MOLPAND Tablet: Water Sigil:

   a. Name: MOLPAND, Moh-leh-pan-deh
   MOLAP-ND can mean "He who receives men"

   b. Gematria: MOLPAND=197=ISRO (promise) = VRELP (an Adept)
   197 is also the Hebrew word TzIMAVN (thirst)

2. VSNARDA Tablet: Water Sigil:

   a. Name: VSNARDA Fes-en-ar-dah
   VS-ADRAN can mean "He who casts down into the depths"

   b. Gematria: VSNARDA=243=SIATRIS (a scorpion)
   243 is also the Hebrew words BRAM (created)
   and GRM (to destroy)
   also 243=81x3, where 81=NAZPS (a sword)
   81 is also the Hebrew ALIM (violence)

3. PONODOL Tablet: Fire Sigil:

a. Name: PONODOL, Poh-noh-doh-leh
PON-OD-OL can mean "He who destroys and creates"

b. Gematria: PONODOL=161=IAIDA-BESZ
(the highest substance)
=TOL-OM (all-knowing)

Location: The 11th Aethyr is situated in the highest subplane conceivable to the human mind, on the brink of the Outer Abyss.

Brief Description: IKH contains a city, sometimes called the Holy City, which represents the highest possible residence for the human mind (*manas*). The entire Aethyr is pervaded by an atmosphere of tension. The proximity of the Abyss gives the feeling of being on a great precipice. There is a strong feeling here that something extremely important is about to occur, although nothing actually happens. The magician who enters here can sometimes see the god Shu. This Egyptian god originally separated the sky (Nut) from the earth (Seb). Here he can be seen separating structured manifestation from the chaotic blackness of the Abyss. The Aethyr also contains vast armies of Angels whose function is to assist Shu and to defend the cosmos from the chaos that encircles it. They keep the mighty Khoronzon in ZAX and prevent him from entering the Aethyrs below the Abyss.

Comment: IKH contains a sense of impending doom. The last vestiges of egoity scream out for survival against the promise of dispersion awaiting in the next Aethyr. The 11th Aethyr marks the last frontier of human consciousness.

THE TENTH AETHYR: ZAX

Name: ZAX is pronounced *Zod-ahtz* and means "The Aethyr of the One with a Great Name."

Gematria: ZAX=415=83x5, where 83=FIFALZ
(to eliminate)
ZAX=409=MALPRG-BITOM
(fiery flames of Fire)
also 409=QUASB-MALPIRG
(destruction of the fires of life)

Governors:

1. LEXARPH   Tablet: Black Cross
   a. Name: LEXARPH,   El-etz-ar-peh-heh
   L-EXARPH can mean "He who is first of the air"
   b. Gematria: LEXARPH=534=KIAOFI-NAZPS
   (terrible sword)
   also 534=276x2, where 267=
   YRPOIL (a division)

2. KOMANAN   Tablet: Black Cross
   a. Name: KOMANAN,   Koh-mah-nah-neh
   K-OM-NANA can mean "He who knows how to manifest"
   b. Gematria: KOMANAN=532=PATRALX
   (stone, rock)=AX-OMA
   (Great Name of Knowledge)

3. TABITOM   Tablet: Black Cross
   a. Name: TABITOM,   Tah-bee-toh-meh
   TA-BITOM can mean "He who is like fire"
   b. Gematria: TABITOM=209=BLIORA (comfort)

209 is also the Hebrew word BZR
(dispersed)
TABITOM = 197 = VRELP
(an Adept) = MOLPAND
(Governor of 11th Aethyr)

Demon of ZAX: KHORONZON

A. Name: KHORONZON is pronounced *Keh-hoh-roh-en-zodoh-en* in seven syllables and means "He who is the basis of form" (KHORO-N-ZON).

b. Gematria: KHORONZON = 600 = OXI-BABALON (mighty evil one)
KHORONZON = 594 = ZIXLAY-GOSA (the confusion of strangeness) also 594 = 54x11, where 54 is the Hebrew word LAAChID (incoherent)

Location: The 10th Aethyr is located at the subplane called the Great Outer Abyss. On the Qabalistic Tree of Life it is called the Veil of the Abyss and separates the three higher Sephiroth from the lower seven.

Brief Description: ZAX is a Ring-Pass-Not for the human mind. It represents an indescribable barrier between phenomena and noumena, matter and spirit. ZAX is the first stage of the Nirvana of Buddhism because it annihilates any ego that enters into it like a great wind blowing out the flame of a lamp. The chief resident in ZAX is the demon Khoronzon. He personifies the forces of dispersion and incoherence, the two primary qualities of this Aethyr. He is sometimes said to be the Master of Form, and he can change shape to suit the magician who dares to enter his domain.

Comment: When the magician enters ZAX, he must relinquish the personal sense of identity. The ego cannot enter ZAX, because Khoronzon will disperse it, and the result will be certain death. The key to this barrier is to meditatively silence the mind in *samadhi* before entering. Consciousness can safely pass through the Abyss so long as it is untainted by personality. The ability to reach a mental state equivalent to samadhi is a prerequisite to the higher Aethyrs.

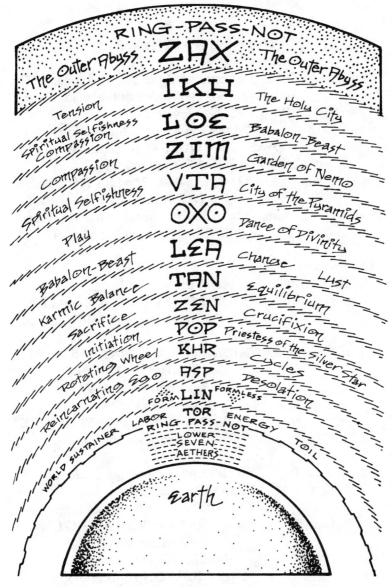

**Figure 29. A Schematic Diagram of the Middle Aethyrs,
From TOR to ZAX.**

THE NINTH AETHYR: ZIP

Name: ZIP is pronounced *Zodee-peh* and means "The Aethyr for those who are not (i.e. void of ego)."

Gematria: ZIP=78=TOTO (cycles)
    also 78x2=156=ARN (2nd Aethyr) and
    78x3=234=QURLST (a handmaiden)
  ZIP=72=TOOAT (to provide)
    also 72=24x3, where 24=LEA (16th Aethyr)
    =PAZ (4th Aethyr)
    and 72x5=360, the number for the Hebrew
    word NShI(feminine, womanly)

Governors:

1. ODDIORG   Tablet: Fire   Sigil:

  a. Name: ODDIORG,   Oh-deh-dee-oh-rah-geh
    OID-OD-RG can mean "He of fire and justice"

  b. Gematria: ODDIORG=236=ENAY BABALON
    (the Lord of Babalon)
    236 is also the Hebrew MTzUQ
    (a cliff)
    also 236=59x4, where 59=BALTOH
    (righteousness)

2. KRALPIR   Tablet: Fire   Sigil:

  a. Name: KRALPIR,   kar-al-pee-ar
    KRAL-PIR can mean "He of bright joy"

  b. Gematria: KRALPIR=583=BOGPA-KHIRLAN
    (to rule with joy)
    also 583=53x11, where 53=
    BALTOH (righteous)
    53 is also the Hebrew word GN
    (garden)

3. DOANZIN   Tablet: Fire   Sigil:

a. Name: DOANZIN,   Doh-an-en-zodee-en
DOAN-ZIN can mean "He who names
the waters"

b. Gematria: DOANZIN=209=TABITOM
(Governor of 10th Aethyr)
DOANZIN=203= BLIOR (comfort)=
PIAMOL (righteousness)

Location: The 9th Aethyr is located directly above the
Abyss on the lowest subplane of the Spiritual Plane.

Brief Description: The magician who rises through the
Abyss will be awed by the beauty and splendor of ZIP.
After leaving the tension of ZAX, the atmosphere of ZIP
will appear like a beautiful garden. In this garden is a
stone palace sometimes called the Stone of the Philoso-
phers and sometimes the Palace of the King's Daughter.
As one enters further into this Aethyr the stone will be
seen as skin and the palace will be seen as the body of an
enormous and beautiful woman. She is known as the
Virgin of Eternity and the Daughter of Babalon. She
personifies the femininity that pervades this Aethyr.
The 9th Aethyr will give one the strong feeling that
spirit is reality and that matter is illusion. *Ananda,* or
bliss, is strong here.

Comment: The 9th Aethyr is very close to the Sephiroth of
Binah on the Tree of Life. The Daughter of Babalon is
the *Shakti* or *Kundalini* of Tantracism, and Isis, the reflex
or "daughter" of the Egyptian goddess Nut. But this is
only one side. She is also the black Kali and the lioness
Sekhet, the dark side of femininity. However, this side
is only hinted at here. The magician will probably do

little more than bask in the bliss of this Aethyr and contemplate the multiple aspects of femininity.

THE EIGHTH AETHYR: ZID

Name: ZID is pronounced *Zodee-deh* and means "The Aethyr of one's [inner] god."

Gematria: ZID=73=GOSAA-ZAH (the stranger within)
73 is also the Hebrew word ChKMH
(wise one, the Sephiroth Chokmah)
ZID=67=ASPT-ADPHAHT
(before the unspeakable)
67 is also the Hebrew word BINH
(understanding, the Sephiroth Binah)

Governors:

1. ZAMFRES   Tablet: Fire   Sigil:
   a. Name: ZAMFRES,   Zodah-em-far-eh-seh
   ZAM-F-RES can mean "He who appears when praised"
   b. Gematria: ZAMFRES=225=EOLIS-
   BABALON (to make evil)
   also 225=15x15, where 15=AP
   (unchanging)=GAH (spirit)
   ZAMFRES=219=ZIRN (wonder)
   also 219=73x3, where 73=ZID
   (8th Aethyr)

2. TODNAON   Tablet: Fire   Sigil:
   a. Name: TODNAON,   Toh-deh-nah-oh-en
   T-OD-NOAN can mean "He who is and who will be"
   b. Gematria: TODNAON=179=BLIAR
   (with comfort)
   TODNAON=173=THARZI (peace)
   also 173x2=346=ZOKHA
   (what is past)

3. PRISTAK   Tablet: Fire   Sigil:

a. Name: PRISTAK,   Peh-ree-seh-tah-keh
               PIR-S-TA-K can mean "He who has the
               likeness of a Holy One"

b. Gematria: PRISTAK = 491 = KALZIRG
               (Governor of 22nd Aethyr)
               PRISTAK = 485 = KALZIRG
               (see 22nd Aethyr)

Location: The 8th Aethyr is located on the Spiritual Plane above the Abyss in the region of one's Holy Guardian Angel. It is between Binah and Chokmah on the Tree of Life, probably somewhere along the 4th path, the Empress.

Brief Description: The Guiding Angel of the 8th Aethyr is one's inner god, the divinity within man. He is sometimes called one's Holy Guardian Angel and his encounter here is known as having "knowledge and conversation with the Holy Guardian Angel." The truth of one's spiritual nature is directly confronted here. The magician who enters ZID must face this truth even though the god usually appears objectively. This Angel will explain one's True Will to each magician who can face him.

Comment: The 8th Aethyr is as masculine as the 9th is feminine. Furthermore the joy that is in ZIP is now serious and sober. Entrance into ZID is the primary goal of all true magic. Only by meeting one's own inner divinity, and thereby learning of one's True Will, can one hope to set about accomplishing that Will.

THE SEVENTH AETHYR: DEO

Name: DEO is pronounced *Deh-oh* and means "The Aethyr of [spiritual] selfishness."

Gematria: DEO=44=OBZA (dual)

44 is also the value of the Hebrew AGM (sorrow)

also 44=22x2, where 22=BALT (justice)

Governors:

1. O^PʙMAKAS   Tablet: Fire   Sigil:

   a. Name: OPMAKAS,   Oh-pah-mah-kah-seh

   O-PAM-KAS can mean "He who is from the beginning"

   b. Gematria: OPMAKAS=448=16x28, where 28= BALT (justice)

   and 16=ATH (works)

   448 is also the Hebrew word MBVQSh (desire)

2. GENADO^Lʙ   Tablet: Fire   Sigil:

   a. Name: GENADOL,   Geh-nah-doh-leh

   GE-ALDON can mean "He who only attracts"

   b. Gematria: GENADOL=116=NIA (24th Aethyr) =MABZA (a robe)

   also 116x3=348, the number for the Hebrew ShMCh (joyful)

3. ASPIAON   Tablet: Fire   Sigil:

   a. Name: ASPIAON,   ah-seh-pee-ah-oh-en

   ASP-IA-ON can mean "He who precedes inner truth"

b. Gematria: ASPIAON=168=BOGPA-BABALON
(the rule of Babalon)
also 168=42x4, where 42 is the Hebrew word AMA
(supernal mother)

Location: DEO is located in the Spiritual Plane where love is predominate. This love takes two forms, love of self (spiritual selfishness) and love of others (compassion).

Brief Description: The 7th Aethyr contains the duality of love for self and love for others. Here love for self is not simple egotism because the ego was left below the Abyss. It is rather the spiritual selfishness embodied by the Pratyeka Buddha, who sees others as *maya* or illusion and therefore has no compassion for them. The Guiding Angel of DEO is a woman who can take many forms. She says, "I am a harlot for such as ravish me, and a virgin with such as know me not." It is this dichotomy that disturbed Edward Kelly when he entered here in the Spirit Vision. The lady of this Aethyr is Venus, goddess of love. She is also the woman portrayed in the Tarot trump called the Star. She is also Sakti, goddess of creative energy. The magician who enters DEO will see the Pratyeka Buddhas that inhabit this Aethyr at the feet of this goddess. They will appear similar to those Adepts in the City of the Pyramids.

Comment: There is a mystical notion that comes to one and says something like, "I am all. There is none but me. I am real and all else is illusion." Some mystics succumb to this idea and think of themselves as a drop of spirit slipping into a spiritual sea. They become Pratyeka Buddhas and occasionally rise all the way to DEO but never farther. The higher Aethyrs are for the Bodhisattvas. The former denies the existence of others. The latter recognizes others and strives to help them to become like himself.

THE SIXTH AETHYR: MAZ

Name: MAZ can be pronounced either *Em-ah-zod* or *Mah-zod* and means "The Aethyr of appearances."

Gematria: MAZ=105=FAONTS (to dwell in)=
ZIZOP (vessels)
105 is also the Hebrew word HPK (change)
also 105=21x5, where 21 is ZAA
(5th Aethyr)=DES (26th Aethyr)
MAZ=99=FAONTS (to dwell in)
99 is also the Hebrew word ChUPH
(vault of Heaven)

Governors:

1. SAXTOMP   Tablet: Fire   Sigil:

   a. Name: SAXTOMP,   Sahtz-toh-em-peh
S-AX-T-OMP can mean "He whose name means understanding"

   b. Gematria: SAXTOMP=551=OM-ZAKARE
(knowledge of motion)
SAXTOMP=545=109x5, where 109=
DOSIG (night)
545 is also the Hebrew MShRH
(end)

2. VA^U_VA^A_IMP   Tablet: Fire   Sigil:

   a. Name: VAUAAMP,   Vah-uah-ah-em-peh
VAU-A-AMP can mean "He who initiates action"

   b. Gematria: VAUAAMP=257=MONONS
(the heart)
257 is also the Hebrew ChRTM
(a magician)

3. ZIRZIRD   Tablet: Fire   Sigil: ⌐
   a. Name: ZIRZIRD, Zodee-rah-zodee-rah-deh
               ZIR-ZIRD can mean "He who was and
               who will be"
   b. Gematria: ZIRZIRD = 342 = HOM-MALPRG
                 (to live in fiery flames)
                 342 is also the Hebrew ShLHBH
                 (flame)
                 ZIRZIRD = 330 = LEVITHMONG
                 (beasts of the field)
                 330 is also the Hebrew words ShL
                 (male) and MRTz (energy)

Location: The 6th Aethyr is situated on the Spiritual Plane in a region which touches the Sephiroth Chokmah on the Tree of Life.

Brief Description: The 6th Aethyr is charged with masculine creative power. As the angel of DEO is feminine, so the angel of MAZ is masculine. He is called Ave (AVE = 86 @ NETAAB (government) by Enochian Gematria). He will show the magician who enters here three types of Adepts who personify the three ways one can look at the world. The yellow Adept is one who is neutral with regard to his environment. He watches it but is not affected by it. The black Adept reacts negatively to his surroundings. He rejects it as illusion or as sorrow. The white Adept reacts positively to his environment. He is joyous and sees all as a delight. These Adepts personify the consciousness-existence-bliss aspects of Brahman. Sometimes Ave will show one the Temple of MAZ. It looks like a huge urn suspended in the air and it contains the ashes of one's past experiences (i.e. one's karmic residue).

Comments: The Temple of MAZ symbolizes that one's karma has been consumed. MAZ is the Aethyr that ends one's personal karma. The magician who can enter MAZ thus becomes a *jivamukti,* one who is "liberated while living."

THE FIFTH AETHYR: LIT

Name: LIT can be pronounced either *Lee-teh* or *El-ee-teh* and means "The Aethyr that is without a supreme being."

Gematria: LIT = 77 = THIL (seat) = ED-NAS (receivers)
            77 is also the Hebrew word SIBH (cause)
            also 77x3 = 231 = IADNAH-MAL
                (knowldge of the arrow)
            LIT = 71 = THIL (seat) = BIA (voice)
            71 is also the Hebrew word ALM (silence)

Governors:

1. LAXDI^{Z}xI Tablet: Water   Sigil:
   a. Name: LAXDIXI,   Lahtz-dee-tzee
                L-AX-DIX-I can mean "He who has no supreme name"
   b. Gematria: LAXDIXI = 938 = PATRALX-AX
                (one whose name is stone)

2. NOKAMAL   Tablet: Water   Sigil:
   a. Name: NOKAMAL,   Noh-kah-mal
                NOKA-MAL can mean "He who is servant of the arrow"
   b. Gematria: NOKAMAL = 490 = OXI (mighty)
                490 is also the Hebrew word
                    ChIVNIVTh (life)

3. TIARPAX   Tablet: Water   Sigil:
   a. Name: TIARPAX,   Tee-ah-rah-pahtz
                T-IARP-AX can mean "He whose name means truth"

b. Gematria: TIARPAX=590=ELO-IPSI-AX
(first holder of a name)
also 590=59x10, where 59=
BALTOH (righteous)
and 10=ATH (works)
TIARPAX=584=IOLKAM-BAGHIE
(to bring forth fury)

Location: The 5th Aethyr is on the Spiritual Plane at a point
where divinity is seen as an endless host of hierarchies.

Brief Description: The 5th Aethyr contains all of the major
gods and goddesses of man. The magician who enters
LIT will see rows of these past and future gods. This
sometimes appears as many avenues of pylons leading
up the side of a mountain. A god or goddess is seated at
each pylon. Following one of these avenues will lead
one to the top of the mountain where the last pylon is
located. Although one would expect the Supreme Deity
to be seated there, an inspection will show that the topmost pylon is empty. There is no Supreme Deity as
such. Over the top of LIT can be seen a huge arrow. This
arrow is sometimes called the Arrow of Truth. It has the
feathers of Maat (goddess of truth), the shaft of Amen
(the "hidden" god) and the barb is the Silver Star of
Isis.

Comment: The 5th Aethyr contains the doctrine of hierarchies. The manifested worlds are created and main-
tained by vast hierarchies of deities. Although each
hierarchy has a chief, or Hierarch, there is no one overall
supreme Hierarch anywhere in the universe. The Arrow
of Truth symbolizes the intelligent forces of guidance
and direction which now replace the concept of a personal Supreme Deity.

THE FOURTH AETHYR: PAZ

Name: PAZ is pronounced *Pah-zod* and means "The Aethyr of impending expression."

Gematria: PAZ=24=LEA (16th Aethyr)=TAFA (poison)
24 is also the Hebrew words AHUBI
(he whom I love)
and AUHBI (he who loves me)
PAZ=18=AFFA (empty)=GE (not)=TAFA
(poison)
18 is also the Hebrew word AHBI
(my beloved)

Governors:

1. THO^T_KAN^F_P Tablet: Water   Sigil:

   a. Name: THOTANF,   Teh-hoh-tah-neff
TOH-TA-N-F can mean "He whose visit means victory"

   b. Gematria: THOTANF=108=BAMS (forget)=
OTHIL (seat)
108 is also the Hebrew word ChNN
(to love very much)
also 108=54x2, where 54=
TALHO (a cup)
THOTANF=96=SONFA
(one who reigns)

2. AX^Z_XIARG   Tablet: Water   Sigil:

   a. Name: AXZIARG,   Ahtz-zodee-ah-rah-geh
AX-Z-IARG can mean "He whose name is Flame"

   b. Gematria: AXZIARG=589=ZIXLAY-GLO
(to stir up things)
AXZIARG=583=53x11, where 53=
BALTOH (righteous)

3. POTHN^I_RR   Tablet: Water   Sigil:

  a. Name: POTHNIR,   Poh-teh-henee-ar
                  P-OTH-NIR can mean "Son of the three-
                  fold throne"

  b. Gematria: POTHNIR=259=T-VABZIR
                       (like an eagle)
                       259 is also the Hebrew word NHDR
                       (lovely)
                       POTHNIR= 253=23x11, where 23 is the
                       Hebrew word ChDVH (joy)

Location: The 4th Aethyr is on the Spiritual Plane in a region which combines femininity and masculinity. It is apparently midway between the two Sephiroths, Binah and Chokmah, but well above the path of the Empress on the Tree of Life.

Brief Description: The magician who enters PAZ will see a combination of femininity and masculinity. This usually takes the form of a beautiful dark woman clinging with arms and legs, to a dark repulsive-looking man. They are clasped in a furious embrace and are obviously hurting each other in the process. She is strangling him while he is trying to tear her apart. A close look will reveal that the dark man is Chaos while the dark woman is another form of Babalon (i.e. the cosmos).

Comment: The struggling woman in PAZ is Cosmos while the man who opposes her is Chaos. By Enochian Gematria, KAOS=343, the number for the Hebrew word ChShIKH (darkness) and KOZMOS=466, the number for the Hebrew word OVLM HITzIRH (the World of Formation). The eternal struggle between Cosmos and Chaos gives rise to the manifested planes and Aethyrs below PAZ. In a magical sense, the man here is the Will while the woman is Love.

THE THIRD AETHYR: ZOM

Name: ZOM is pronounced *Zod-oh-em* and means "The Aethyr of self-knowledge."

Gematria: ZOM=129=MOZ (joy)
              129 is also the Hebrew word ODNH
                      (pleasure, delight)
              ZOM=123=MOZ= (joy)
              123 is also the Hebrew word ONG
                      (pleasure, delight)

Governors:

1. **SAMAPHA**   Tablet: Water   Sigil:
    a. Name: SAMAPHA,   Sah-mah-peh-hah
                  SA-M-APHA can mean "He who is with continuity"
    b. Gematria: SAMAPHA=125=LRASD
                      (to dispose of)
                125 is also the Hebrew word KPIIH
                      (a force)

2. **VIR$^{\text{l}}_{\text{k}}$OLI**   Tablet: Water   Sigil:
    a. Name: VIRLOLI,   Vee-rah-loh-lee
                  VIR-L-OLI can mean "He who made the first nest"
    b. Gematria: VIRLOLI=336=LEVITHMONG
                      (beasts of the field)
                336 is also the Hebrew words
                MKVOR (ugly) and ROIVN (thought)

3. **A$^{\text{N}}_{\text{A}}$DISPI**   Tablet: Water   Sigil:
    a. Name: ANADISPI,   Ah-nah-dee-ess-pee
                  ADNA-IPZI can mean "He who binds into obedience"

b. Gematria: ANADISPI=202=AMMA-ATH
(cursed works)
202 is also the Hebrew words BR
(pure) and BQQ (to make empty)

Location: The 3rd Aethyr is on the Spiritual Plane along the second path of the Tree of Life, the Magician, Magus, or Juggler.

Brief Description: The magician who enters ZOM will become a Magus. In ZOM one will learn that all objective reality is intimately connected to the subjective self. The monadic essence of man contains an infinitesimal consciousness center and its infinite universe. In short, man is a circle whose center is nowhere and whose circumference is everywhere. In ZOM the magician will learn how to consciously control his surroundings as well as himself. In the 8th Aethyr, the magician learned his True Will. In ZOM he learns how to carry it out. One who enters ZOM can become a Maker of Illusions because he will learn how to be consciously creative. The Aethyr is permeated by a feeling of creative freedom.

Comment: ZOM is the Aethyr of self-knowledge. The experiences gained here can make one a Magus, the highest of Adepts. Here the magician will see that his True Will is nothing less than the full conscious expression of his inherent qualitites and characteristics through the planes and Aethyrs. The Magus in ZOM is like an artist who realizes that he is completely free to paint whatever kind of picture he wants so long as he lets other artists do the same.

THE SECOND AETHYR: ARN

Name: ARN is pronounced *Ar-en* and means "The Aethyr of fulfillment."

Gematria: ARN = 156 = OLPRT (light) =
LONSHI (power)
= No. of squares in each Tablet
and 156 = GLO-BABALON
(the things of Babalon)
also 156 = 78x2, where 78 = ZIP
(9th Aethyr)

Governors:

1. DO^NAGNIS   Tablet: Water   Sigil:

   a. Name: DOAGNIS,   Doh-ah-geh-nee-seh
   DO-AG-NIS can mean "He who comes
   without a name"
   b. Gematria: DOAGNIS = 165 = L-ZORGE
   (first love)
   165 is also the Hebrew OMMIH
   (Master of the Temple)
   also 165 = 55x3, where 55 is the Hebrew KLH (bride)

2. PAKASNA   Tablet: Water   Sigil:

   a. Name: Pah-kah-ess-nah
   AP-KASNA can mean "He who is unchanged by time"
   b. Gematria: PAKASNA = 384 = 48x8, where 48 =
   TALHO (cup)
   48 is also the Hebrew word ChIL
   (a woman)
   and 8 is the Hebrew word DD
   (love)

3. DIAIᵛoIA   Tablet: Water   Sigil:

   a. Name: DIAIVOIA,   Dee-ah-ee-voh-ee-ah
                   IAD-I-VO-IA can mean "The god where
                   truth is"

   b. Gematria: DIAIVOIA = 296 = AR-QUASAHI
                   (delight in the sun)
                   also 296 = 148x2, where 148 =
                   ORSBA (intoxicated)

Location: The 2nd Aethyr is close to the top of the Spiritual Plane. It is the region of Babalon.

Brief Description: ARN is the home of the mysterious BABALON who was first seen in LEA, and whose daughter was seen in ZIP. Here she is seen directly and completely. The vision is indescribable. A hint is given in the name itself because BAB-ALON can mean "the attraction of sound." She is in fact a personification of the powerful force of attraction that exists between the subjective self and the objective non-self. The ancient Egyptians symbolized the self as a winged globe (a form of Horus) and the not-self as the goddess Nut (Space), who was shown arched over the world in the form of the night sky. All of these ideas will be encountered in ARN in one form or another. The entire atmosphere of ARN is characterized by intense bliss.

Comment: The direction of the Aethyrs is towards non-duality. Each is slightly more non-dual than the other until LIL, the highest of thirty Aethyrs and the first stage of true non-duality. In ARN the ultimate duality (all of the others are expressions or offshoots of this one) of subject and object is confronted. This results in the highest form of *samadhi,* called *nirvikalpa* in Vedanta. The struggle of PAZ is now a gentle and loving sharing.

THE FIRST AETHYR: LIL

Name: LIL can be pronounced either *El-ee-el* or *Lee-el* and means "The first Aethyr."

Gematria: LIL=76=TABAAN
(governor, ruler)
76 is also the Hebrew words ChBIUN
(secret place)
and NIChCh (peace)
also 76=38x2, where 38=OL (maker)
38 is also the Hebrew ZKAI (innocent)

Governors:

1. OKKODON   Tablet: Water   Sigil:
   a. Name: OKKODON,   Oh-keh-koh-doh-en
   KOKO-DO-N can mean "He whose name is Renewal"
   b. Gematria: OKKODON=744=KIKLE-TOTO
   (mysteries of cycles)
   also 744=93x8, where 93=TOL-QAA (all of creation)

2. PA^x_sKOMB   Tablet: Water   Sigil:
   a. Name: PASKOMB,   Pah-ess-koh-em-beh
   PAS-K-OMB can mean "He who precedes understanding"
   b. Gematria: PASKOMB=447=KRAL-PAGE
   (joyous rest)
   also 447=148x3, where 149=
   T-TIANTA (like a bed)
   149 is also the Hebrew DLIQH
   (fire) and KVCh HDMIVN
   (imagination)

211

3. VALGARS   Tablet: Water   Sigil:

    a. Name: VALGARS,   Val-gar-ess

              VAL-G-ARS can mean "He who works with that which is"

    b. Gematria: VALGARS = 205 = NIBM (season) = PARM (to run, to flow)

              205 is also the Hebrew words GBR (man) and HR (mountain)

Location: The first Aethyr is the highest region conceivable to the human spirit. It is located at the apex of the Spiritual Plane just below a Ring-Pass-Not for the spirit.

Brief Description: LIL is the first stage of non-duality. Its symbol is a little child or babe, the embodiment of innocence and purity. As ARN is the Aethyr of Babalon, so LIL is the Aethyr of the beast. But the unruly beast of the lower Aethyrs is now tamed and is changed into a child. This child represents the fruition of the Great Work. The ancient Egyptians embodied this idea in Hor-pa-Khrat or Harpocrates, the child Horus.

Comment: LIL is the highest Aethyr possible for man to enter and still be able to return to talk about it. Beyond LIL is the realm of non-dual divinity about which nothing can be said.

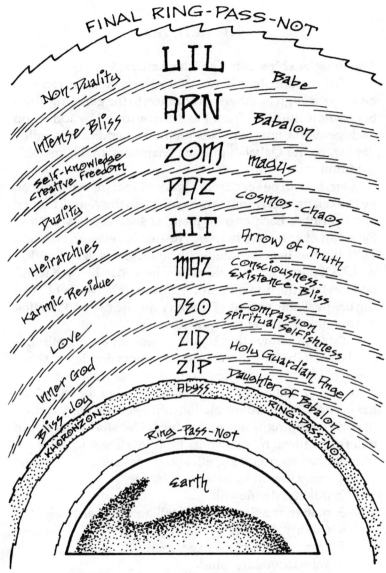

FINAL RING-PASS-NOT

LIL
Non-Duality — Babe
ARN
Intense Bliss — Babalon
ZOM
Self-knowledge
creative Freedom — magus
PAZ
Duality — cosmos-chaos
LIT
Heirarchies — Arrow of Truth
MAZ
Karmic Residue — Consciousness-
Existence-Bliss
DEO
Love — compassion
spiritual selfishness
ZID
Inner God — Holy Guardian Angel
ZIP
Daughter of Babalon
Bliss-Joy — Abyss — RING-PASS-NOT
KHORONZON

Ring-Pass-Not

Earth

Figure 30. A Schematic Diagram of the Highest Aethyrs, from ZIP to LIL.

213

THE AETHYRS

The Relationships Between The Aethyrs.

The relationships between the thirty Aethyrs can best be seen through numbers. In addition to the gematria numbers, whole numbers from 1 to 8 can be found by adding up each gematria number. This method of addition is called *Aiq Bkr*, or the Qabalah of Nine chambers, or Theosophic Addition.

First, it can be seen from Figure 31 that the Aethyrs can be broken up nicely into three groups; in the Astral, Mental and Spiritual. Each cosmic plane is separated by a Ring-Pass-Not or spherical barrier. The first is between NIA and TOR and this bars the intellect. The second is between IKH and ZAX (although it could as well be said to be ZAX itself) and this bars the human mind. The third is between LIL and the unspeakable realms of divinity that lie beyond the first Aethyr and this bars the human spirit.

Table IX shows the *Aiq Bkr* values for each Aethyr. It can be seen that the three Ring-Pass-Nots divide the thirty Aethyrs into three groups each of whose total numerical value can be reduced to 7, the occult number for completeness. There is a hidden relationship between each Aethyr of corresponding numerical values. The student is left to determine these relationships for himself. As an aid, each number has an occult significance as follows:

1   unity, oneness, extension, spirit
2   duality, divine will
3   matter, manifestation, intelligence, space
4   solidity, firmness, time
5   spirit and matter mixed, man
6   animation, life, mind
7   completeness, wholeness, satisfaction
8   cycles, spirals

It should be noted that the only Aethyr with a value of

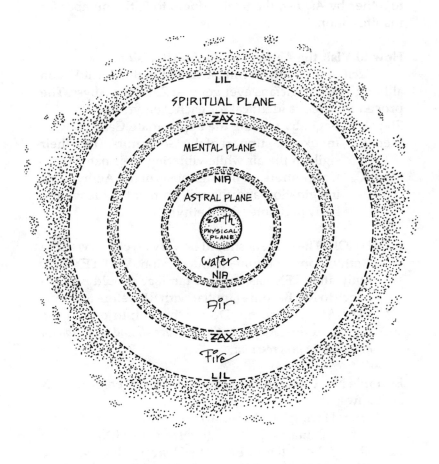

Figure 31. The Ring-Pass-Nots of the Thirty Aethyrs.

2 is TAN, the Aethyr of the Great Balance. Also, no Aethyr has the number 9. Finally, if all thirty Aethyrs are added together by *Aiq Bkr*, the total reduces to 3, the number for manifestation.

How to Visit the Aethyrs in the Spirit Vision.

Each of the Aethyrs can be visited in the Spirit Vision although few magicians ever get past ZAX, the Abyss. The procedure used is identical for each Aethyr.

Step 1. Begin by reciting the appropriate Call.

Step 2. Invoke the support of the Governors. Trace their sigils in the air while vibrating their names.

Step 3. Concentrate on the signposts of the Aethyr. Use imagination and the will to mentally leave the body and enter the Aethyr.

A CAUTION. The student should be very careful to visit the Aethyrs one at a time, in succession. Visit TEX first. Only after TEX has become familiar should one advance to RII. Become familiar with RII before attempting BAG, and so on. Do not jump into one of the higher Aethrs. *Rising in the Aethyrs should be a gradual and orderly progression.*

Example No. 1. The student should begin by entering TEX as follows:

1. Stand facing North (i.e. face the Watchtower of Water which contains the four governors of TEX).

2. Recite the Call for TEX: "The Heavens that are in the Thirtieth Aethyr, TEX, are mighty in those regions of the universe ... " etc.

3. Vibrate the names MPH-ARSL-GAIOL and RAAGIOL.

4. Vibrate the name TAOAGLA and trace his sigil in the air. The sigil should be blue, the color of the Watch-

TABLE IX. USING AIQ BKR WITH THE AETHYRS

No.	Name	Numerical Value	
		Gematria	Aiq Brk
30	TEX	413	8
29	RII	220	4
28	BAG	19	1
27	ZAA	21	3
26	DES	21	3
25	VTI	133	7
24	NIA	116	8
	Totals	943	7
	RING-PASS-NOT		
23	TOR	133	7
22	LIN	118	1
21	ASP	22	4
20	KHR	401	5
19	POP	48	3
18	ZEN	69	6
17	TAN	65	2
16	LEA	24	6
15	OXO	460	1
14	VTA	79	7
13	ZIM	159	6
12	LOE	48	3
11	IKH	361	1
	Totals	1996	7
	RING-PASS-NOT		
10	ZAX	415	1
9	ZIP	78	6
8	ZID	73	1
7	DEO	44	8
6	MAZ	105	6
5	LIT	77	5
4	PAZ	24	6
3	ZOM	129	3
2	ARN	156	3
1	LIL	76	4
	Totals	1177	7
	RING-PASS-NOT		

tower. This Governor is kindly and righteous. He rules in the subquadrant Air of Water.

5. Vibrate the name GEMNIMB and trace his sigil in blue. This Governor is very judgmental, but his judgments are temporary and can be changed. He rules in the subquadrant Water of Water.

6. Vibrate the name ADUORPT and trace his sigil in blue. This governor is feminine and passive like the moon. She rules in the subquadrant Air of Water and Water of Water, partaking of both.

7. Vibrate the name DOZIAAL and trace his sigil in blue. This Governor is very emotional and he can bestow either pleasure or pain, joy or sorrow. He rules in the subquadrant Water of Water.

8. Concentrate on TEX, a region of four sections:
   a.   TAOAGLA governs the North.
   b.   GEMNIMB governs the East.
   c.   ADUORPT governs the South.
   d.   DOZIAAL governs the West.

9. Meditate on each of the four Governors and their attributes. Try to see the Aethyr divided by karma, desire, silence and restriction. The inhabitants of the North will be mainly governed by their karma. Those of the East will mainly be controlled by their desires. Those in the South will largely be quiet and reflective. Those in the West will, for the most part, be like captives; bound by their own sense of limitations.

Example No. 2. After experience is gained in TEX, the student can try to enter RII as follows:

1. Stand facing South (i.e. face the Watchtower of Earth that contains the three Governors of RII).

2. Recite the Call for RII: "The Heavens that are in the twenty-ninth Aethyr, RII, are mighty in those regions of the universe . . . " and so on.

3. Vibrate the names MOR-DIAL-HKTGA and IKZHIKAL.
4. Vibrate the name VASTRIM and trace his sigil in the air. The sigil should be black, the color of the Watchtower of Earth (this sigil is a straight line going from left to right). This Governor is ugly to look at but his nature is merciful. He rules mainly in the subquadrant Fire of Earth but also slightly in Earth of Earth.
5. Vibrate the name ODRAXTI and trace his sigil in black. This Governor has the power to create and destroy and he does both according to his strong sense of justice. He rules in the subquadrant Earth of Earth.
6. Vibrate the name GMOTZIAM and trace her black sigil in the air. This Governor is a personification of self-love and self-concern. She rules in the subquadrant Fire of Fire.
7. Concentrate of RII, a region divided into four sections: judgment, purgatory, heaven, and stagnation. The three Governors overlap all four sections.
8. Meditate on each of the three Governors and their attributes of mercy, justice and selfishness. Try to see the Aethyr and its inhabitants; those deceased persons who are awaiting judgment, those who are being judged after death, and those who have already been judged, as well as those who are in a mental stupor and who refuse to acknowledge what is happening to them.

Example No. 3. After experience is gained in TEX and RII, the student can try to enter BAG as follows:
1. Face South, recite the Call for the twenty-eighth Aethyr, BAG, and vibrate MOR-DIAL-HKTGA and IKZHIKAL as in Example No. 2.
2. Vibrate the name TABNIXP and trace his black sigil in the air. This Governor likes to put labels on everyone who enters BAG. He labels most of the inhabitants as

sinners. He rules in the subquadrant Fire of Earth.

3. Vibrate the name FOKLSNI and trace his black sigil in the air. This Governor visits the inhabitants of BAG and brings forth those he deems to be worthy. He rules in the subquadrant Earth of Earth and Fire of Earth.

4. Vibrate the name OXLOPAR and trace his sigil in black. This Governor has the power to control the inhabitants of BAG due to their own sense of unworthiness. He knows their personal past histories and uses this to manipulate them. He rules in the subquadrant Earth of Earth.

5. Concentrate on BAG, a region permeated by feelings of unworthiness and doubt and a tendency towards self-pity. The inhabitants of BAG have rather low opinions of themselves and do not feel worthy of the higher Aethyrs.

Note. The remaining Aethyrs can be visited in the same way as the above examples. Remember that all sigils of Governors in the Watchtower of Air are all yellow. The only exception is in ZAX where the Governors have no sigils.

A SPIRIT VISION WORK SHEET

It is a good idea to make up a work sheet for each operation. Such a work sheet should contain all of the major elements that you should need for your operation and would serve three primary functions:

(1) **Preparation.** It will allow you to prepare yourself for the operation beforehand by familiarization with the material and its goal in your mind.

(2) **Data Base.** It will serve as a source of information, a data base, when you record your results in your diary and plan for future operations.

(3) **Structure.** It will help structure each operation in a way that is magically progressive and spiritually rewarding because it will force you to learn something from each operation.

Each student is advised to use a work sheet such as the one shown on page 223. This is a general work sheet that can be used for Spirit Visions in the Watchtowers or Aethyrs. If you like, you can tailor each sheet to fit your specific operation. They should be used in a scientific manner. The purpose is to faithfully record as much information as you can. You won't know what is important until these sheets are analyzed at a later time. Meanwhile, always record as much data as you can. After a series of operations, you will be able to go over these sheets and look for patterns and messages which can indicate your progress in Enochian Magic. For example, you may find that you got poor results on days when your health was also poor. You may find that on some days of the week or certain periods of the month you recorded better results than at other times. By experimenting with weapons and preparations you are almost certain to find a combination that works well for you. You may discover that some regions are easier to visit than others, you may learn more in some regions than in others,

221

and so on. Results of such self-analyses will show you your own biorythmic cycles with regard to Magic and will help you to measure your own progress, or lack of progress. All beginners will have periodic good results and poor results. The important thing is to find your own cycles and to determine the preparations and times that work best for you.

SPIRIT VISION WORK SHEET

1. Region to be visited:
   a.   Aethyr
   b.   Square

2. Purpose/Goal of operation:

3. Date of operation:

4. Time of operation:

5. Place of operation:

6. General physical health:

7. Magical weapons/instruments:

8. Preparations for operation:

9. Call(s) recited:

10. Names of Power for operation:

Watchtowers	Aethyrs
a. Great Holy Name	a. Aethyr name
b. King	b. Governors
c. Seniors	(1) Names
d. Archangel	(2) Sigils
e. Angel	

11. Major signposts for operation:
    a.
    b.
    c.
    d.

12. Hazards to avoid:

13. Results:
    a. Was the goal obtained?

    b. Problems encountered:

    c. Beings encountered:

    d. Lessons learned:

    e. Things to do differently next time:

CHIEF HAZARDS OF THE AETHYRS

In addition to the normal hazards associated with Astral Projection and Rising on the Planes, each Aethyr is associated with special dangers for the unwary magician. Awareness of these pitfalls beforehand can prevent unnecessary sorrow.

1. TEX, RII, BAG and ZAA all contain the typical hazards of the Astral Plane. The primary danger is to mistake illusion for reality. The magician in these Aethyrs is apt to use psychic projection unconsciously and thereby mistake a fantasy for a fact. The only remedy for this problem is to eliminate one's personal emotions and ego-oriented desires (a task of many lifetimes). The astral body (i.e. one's emotions and personal feelings) must be clear if one wishes to see through it clearly. Use known signposts as guides against an overly fanciful imagination. Another hazard in these Aethyrs is one's karma. The four lower Aethyrs are highly karmic and many seeds will be germinated from any Spirit Vision there. There is no effective prevention from this hazard. Everyone must work out his own karma sooner or later and in his own fashion.

2. DES suggests to everyone who enters there that the logic and reason of the human mind can eventually solve all problems and resolve all conflicts. This enticement is like a snare in that it tends to hold one in the region with no hope of ever going on to the higher Aethyrs. Logic and reason can go no higher than DES.

3. VTI tends to bring about spiritual pride which is self-limiting.

4. NIA includes Astral Traveling, which is itself dangerous. The "price" that one must pay to enter NIA is death to the "old" personality. One must be willing to be reborn. This idea of death and rebirth is closely associated with the process of initiation, which is emphasized in most of the

Aethyrs.

5. In order to rise above NIA into TOR consciousness must pass through the first Ring-Pass-Not. This is a barrier to the astral body. NIA is the highest region attainable in the astral body. TOR must be entered in the mental body. One's personal feelings, emotions and reactions must be put aside. TOR suggests the serious nature of life and the tedious business of maintaining life. The danger in TOR is a lack of joy and of perhaps taking life a little too seriously.

6. LIN is the first "mystical" Aethyr and is entered by approaching a mental state known in the East as *samadhi*. Most of the typical dangers associated with mystical experiences are also met in LIN. One must be able to change long-held viewpoints about life while retaining sanity and perspective. The human mind sees LIN as a region of cold desolation. Intuitive insight must be used to see that formlessness is not annihilation.

7. The sense of desolation in LIN is intensified in ASP and so the possibility of despair is greater. In ASP the personality sees that it is but one of countless expressions in time and space of an Oversoul or Reincarnating Ego. If not previously prepared for this direct encounter, extensive psychic damage is not only possible, but likely.

8. In KHR the whole world can be seen as either an enticing opportunity for experience or as a deceptive bondage. The danger is to see only one side while rejecting the other. The best preventative remedy for KHR is a good sense of humor.

9. POP and ZEN are both initiatory and require special preparation in order for safe passage. Both can lead to psychological damage for the uninitiated.

10. TAN contains the karmic balance of the universe. The primary hazard in TAN is the possibility of obtaining a false sense of morality. One's entire standard of ethics and morals is rooted in TAN.

11. LEA provides the first opportunity to see Babalon and to experience the lustful attraction of the subjective self with the objective world. The alluring and sultry nature of Babalon is a hazard to anyone who enters LEA with unfulfilled desires. There is a strong sexual force in the atmosphere of LEA which the magician must learn to control.

12. OXO, like LEA, contains a sexual force which the magician must learn to cope with. In OXO the force is clearly a reflex of *ananda,* spiritual bliss. The magician will encounter symbols charged with strong sexual content such as the *lingam* and *yoni* of Hinduism and Tantra. One of the dangers in OXO is the addictive nature of joy there.

13. The chief danger encountered in VTA is the tendency to become one of the countless pyramid-like Adepts who inhabit the City of the Pyramids. Those yogis who have suppressed their desires and attachments while retaining the ego, easily become trapped in VTA.

13. ZIM, LOE and IKH all concern the development of compassion and all are preparatory to the Abyss of ZAX. The ego must be put aside. Failure to do so can be fatal when entering ZAX. There are several ways of silencing the ego. One is compassion for others and this is the preferred method. Another is to see oneself as a spiritual being or Ego and the human ego as an illusion or social fiction. The magical operation required for safe entrance into ZAX is to shift the sense of identity from the human to the divine. In occult terms, one must raise consciousness from the mental body to the spiritual body. The Demon Khoronzon will tear all aggragates down to their smallest constituent components. Nothing with form or structure can get by him. But consciousness itself is formless and is unaffected by Khoronzon. The magician must visualize himself as a geometric point of consciousness; a monad. He must cast aside the human mind (the mental body) and function in the Body of Light, the spiritual body. This body is a monadic sphere of con-

sciousness. It is an understatement to say that this is not easy and that few Adepts can safely enter ZAX. The magician who stands in IKH facing ZAX is equivalent to one who positions his consciousness so that it faces the darkness of the subconscious.

15. ZIP, DEO, PAZ and ARN are all highly charged with feminine force. All four Aethyrs have sexual elements which can snare the uninititiated.

16. ZID, MAZ, LIT and ZOM are all highly charged with masculine force. All four Aethyrs deal with the nature of consciousness and its affect upon the universe. Each requires a high degree of awareness and control.

17. LIL is the highest of the known Aethyrs but not the highest of all possible Aethyrs. The Aethyrs above LIL cannot be visited by any known magical operation, but can be inferred, by analogy and correspondences, to be endless. The feeling of supremacy in LIL is deceptive.

THE NINETY-TWO GOVERNORS:
THEIR PRIMARY FUNCTIONS

The details of each Governor will vary with the magician, but in general, the following can be used as signposts through the Aethyrs:

30. TEX
   a. TAOAGLA (Tah-oh-ah-geh-lah) is a kindly but stern judge like a concerned father. He seeks to keep things in their proper places.
   b. GEMNIMB (Gem-nee-em-bah) is a flexible judge who is quick to make decisions but is willing to change them later if necessary.
   c. ADUORPT (Ah-du-oh-rah-peh-teh) is a passive judge who is slow to make decisions and who usually goes along with the other Governors.
   d. DOZIAAL (doh-zodee-ah-ah-leh) is a cruel judge who takes delight in pain and karmic suffering.

29. RII
   a. VASTRIM (Vah-seh-tah-ree-em) is a merciful judge who seeks to carry out the necessities of karma for all those who enter RII.
   b. ODRAXTI (Oh-dar-ahtz-tee) assigns residents of RII to their karmic destinies.
   c. GMOTZIAM (Geh-moh-teh-zodee-ah-meh) causes the residents of RII to emphasize their self-concerns such as self-love or self-hate, pride or pity.

28. BAG
   a. TABNIXP (Tah-ben-eetz-peh) is a Governor who names (i.e. puts labels on) everyone who enters BAG.
   b. FOKLSNI (Foh-kel-ess-nee) visits everyone who enters BAG and causes them to dwell upon their

guilts and sense of unworthiness.

c. OXLOPAR (Ohtz-loh-par) attempts to control those who enter BAG by means of their own sense of guilt and sinfulness.

27. ZAA

a. SAZIAMI (Sah-zodee-ah-mee) bestows the power to control the elements on all who enter ZAA.

b. MATHVLA (Mah-teh-hev-lah) gives a sense of desolation, inertness, and stagnation to all who enter ZAA.

c. KORPANIB (Koh-ar-pah-nee-beh) gives all who enter ZAA the ability to speak with thoughts, to go beyond the need for words, to communicate telepathically.

26. DES

A. POPHAND (Poh-peh-hah-en-deh) causes division and divisiveness between the intellect (solar) and the intuition (lunar).

b. NIGRANA (Nee-gar-ah-nah) governs the intuition and assails the logic and reason of the intellect.

c. BAZHIIM (Bah-zod-hee-ee-meh) dims the intellectual faculty of all who enter DES by using it against itself.

25. VTI

a. MIRZIND (Mee-rah-zodee-en-deh) slays the intellect of all who enter VTI.

b. OBVAORS (Oh-beh-vah-oh-ress) gives safety and comfort to the intuition.

c. RANGLAM (Rah-neh-geh-lah-meh) assists all who enter VTI to control their higher mind *(buddhimanas)* while silencing their lower mind *(kamamanas)*.

24. NIA

a. ORAKIMIR (Oh-rah-kah-mee-ar) bestows mobility on all who enter NIA.

b. KHIASALPS (Keh-hee-ah-sal-pess) bestows a sense of joy.

c. SOAGEEL (Soh-ah-geh-el) assists those who enter NIA to assimilate all of the experiences encountered in the lower seven Aethyrs.

23. TOR

a. RONOAMB (Roh-noh-ah-meh-beh) is a tireless protector of the lower Aethyrs and of the Earth.

b. ONIZIMP (Oh-nee-zodee-em-peh) emphasizes the love of honest labor.

c. ZAXANIN (Zod-ahtz-ah-nee-en) is a creator who solidifies ideas by converting spirit into matter.

22. LIN

a. OZIDAIA (Oh-zodee-dah-ee-ah) bestows joy and mercy on all who enter LIN and seeks to convert all form into its formless essence.

b. LAZDIXR (Lah-zodee-tzar) bestows joy on all who enter LIN, and gives them a sense of delight as formless essence takes on form.

c. KALZIRG (Kal-zodee-ar-geh) bestows joy on all who enter LIN and seeks to convert all formless essence into those forms which express them.

d. PARAOAN (Pah-rah-oh-ah-en) bestows joy on all who enter LIN and allows them to see form being converted into its formless essence.

21. ASP

a. KHLIRZPA (Keh-helee-rah-zod-pah) delights in the death of the personality and seeks to sacrifice the personality for the individuality behind it.

b. TOANTOM (Toh-ah-en-toh-em) bestows the knowledge of the Reincarnating Ego to all who enter ASP.

c. VIXPALG (Veetz-pah-leh-geh) destroys the personality of anyone who enters ASP. No one can confront this Governor and remain the same.

20. KHR
a. ZILDRON (Zodee-el-dar-oh-en) maintains the circuit of the universe and so appears as a perpetual creator.

b. PARZIBA (Par-zodee-bah) maintains the harmony of the wheel-like universe and also appears as a perpetual creator.

c. TOTOKAN (Toh-toh-kan) maintains the cycles of the universe at selected intervals and so appears as a periodic creator.

19. POP
a. TORZOXI (Toh-razod-oh-tzee) assists all who enter POP to face up to, and understand the meaning of, death.

b. ABRAIOND (Ah-bar-ahee-oh-en-deh) assists all who enter POP to face up to, and understand the meaning of, discord and sorrow.

c. OMAGRAP (Oh-mah-gar-ah-peh) is a teacher of lunar knowledge who assists all who enter POP to overcome fear, especially fear of death.

18. ZEN
a. NABAOMI (Nah-bah-oh-mee) is a Master of the Lunar Current who assists all who enter ZEN to overcome pain and suffering.

b. ZAFASAI (Zodah-fah-sahee) is a Master of Space who will assist all who enter ZEN to understand the meaning of Emptiness.

c. VALPAMB (Val-pah-meh-beh) is a Master of Time who will assist all who enter ZEN to understand the beginning and the end of all things.

17. TAN

a. SIGMORF (See-geh-moh-rah-feh) bestows justice tempered with mercy.

b. AYDROPT (Ah-yeh-deh-roh-peh-teh) bestows a passive sense of equality.

c. TOKARZI (Toh-kar-zodee) bestows the knowledge of equality and cycles to all who enter TAN.

16. LEA

a. KUKUARPT (Ku-ku-rah-peh-teh) is beautiful and sexually attractive and will bestow bliss, but will also bring out any unfulfilled desires, especially those of a sexual nature.

b. LAUAKON (Lah-u-ah-koh-en) will promise happiness and bliss to all who enter LEA, but only as a function of time (i.e. in the future).

c. SOKHIAL (Soh-keh-hee-al) will consume much of the past karma of anyone who enters LEA and will bestow a new sense of self, one that is spiritual.

15. OXO

a. TAHAMDO (Tah-hah-meh-doh) bestows a new viewpoint, one of honesty and clarity; the ability to accept outward things and events as they really are, without bias or prejudice.

b. NOKIABI (Noh-kee-ah-bee) bestows a new viewpoint, one of honesty and clarity; the ability to accept inward thoughts and emotions as they really are without bias or prejudice.

c. TASTOXO (Tah-seh-toh-tzoh) bestows a joy of life, a delightful acceptance of things and events, the viewpoint that all manifested existence is the dance of divinity.

14. VTA

a. TEDOAND (Teh-doh-ah-en-deh) bestows the capacity for passive obedience and introspection on all who enter VTA.

b. VIVIPOS (Vee-vee-poh-seh) gives all who enter VTA a sense of cyclic transiency; all things must end, but all endings are also beginnings.

c. VOANAMB (Voh-ah-nah-em-beh) bestows the ability to see that all things and events are relative to an observer.

13. ZIM

a. GEKAOND (Geh-kah-oh-en-deh) activates the magical memory for all who enter ZIM and emphasizes obedience to law.

b. LAPARIN (Lah-pah-ree-en) is a protector of those who have earned the right to enter ZIM, but will slay those who try to enter prematurely.

c. DOKEPAX (Doh-keh-pahtz) judges the capabilities of those who enter ZIM and assigns duties accordingly.

12. LOE

a. TAPAMAL (Tah-pah-mal) intimately receives all who enter LOE and seeks to show them their true selves, without ego-tainted illusions.

b. GEDOONS (Geh-doh-oh-ness) assists those who enter LOE to prepare for the Abyss by eliminating the ego.

c. AMBRIOL (Ah-em-beh-ree-oh-leh) bestows safety and comfort on those who have eliminated egoism.

11. IKH

a. MOLPAND (Moh-el-pan-deh) receives all who enter IKH, seeks to quench any unfulfilled desires, and promises adeptship for any who can safely enter ZAX.

b. VSNARDA (Vess-en-ar-dah) assists those in IKH who can face the Abyss of ZAX but slays those who are unprepared.

c. PONODOL (Poh-noh-doh-leh) shows those who enter IKH how the lower Aethyrs are created and destroyed.

10. ZAX

a. LEXARPH (El-etz-ar-peh-heh) reduces all formed aggragates entering ZAX from IKH into their form-less monadic components.

b. KOMANAN (Koh-mah-nah-neh) combines the form-less monadic particles entering ZAX from ZIP into formed aggragates.

c. TABITOM (Tah-bee-toh-meh) is like a consuming fire and can either comfort or burn depending upon one's preparedness.

9. ZIP

a. ODDIORG (Oh-deh-dee-oh-rah-geh) is like a kar-mic fire and purifies all those who enter ZIP.

b. KRALPIR (Kar-al-pee-ar) bestows intense joy and bliss on those who enter the garden of ZIP.

c. DOANZIN (Doh-ah-en-zodee-en) offers safety and comfort to those in ZIP.

8. ZID

a. ZAMFRES (Zodah-em-far-eh-seh) is wondrous and offers guidance to all who enter ZID.

b. TODNAON (Toh-deh-nah-oh-en) is timeless and offers peace.

c. PRISTAK (Peh-ree-seh-tah-keh) is holy and offers joy and safety.

7. DEO

a. OPMAKAS (Oh-peh-mah-kah-seh) is an Ancient One who fulfills karmic desires by germinating the karmic seeds of those who enter DEO.

b. GENADOL (Geh-nah-doh-leh) gathers together those who see only themselves (i.e. Pratyeka Buddhas).

c. ASPIAON (Ah-seh-pee-ah-oh-en) is like a mother for all who enter DEO.

6. MAZ

a. SAXTOMP (Sahtz-toh-em-peh) bestows that spiritual understanding which consumes karma.

b. VAUAAMP (Vah-uah-ah-em-peh) shows all who enter MAZ the relationship between the subjective self and the objective world, in terms of the actions and reactions between the two.

c. ZIRZIRD (Zodee-rah-zodee-rah-deh) assists the inhabitants of MAZ to consume their remaining karma in the fires of purification.

5. LIT

a. LAXDIXI (Lahtz-dee-tzee) teaches all who enter LIT the doctrine of hierarchies, that there is no *supreme* being except in a relative sense.

b. NOKAMAL (Noh-kah-mal) shows all who enter LIT the mighty Arrow of Truth and initiates them into its meaning.

c. TIARPAX (Tee-ah-rah-pahtz) teaches all who enter LIT that truth is relative, that existence is open-ended and that there are no absolutes.

4. PAZ

a. THOTANF (Teh-hoh-tah-neff) teaches all who enter PAZ of the victory of Cosmos (KOZMOS) over Chaos (KAOS) and of their endless loving attraction for each other.

b. AXZIARG (Ahtz-zodee-ah-rah-geh) teaches all who enter PAZ of the eventual consumation of Cosmos (KOSMOZ) by Chaos (KAOS) and of their endless loving attraction for each other.

c. POTHNIR (Poh-teh-henee-ar) teaches all who enter PAZ of the beautiful and joyous struggle between Cosmos (KOSMOS) and Chaos (KAOS).

3. ZOM

a. SAMAPHA (Sah-mah-peh-hah) teaches all who enter ZOM how to maintain continuity of consciousness and how to control consciousness.

b. VIRLOLI (Vee-rah-loh-lee) is the initiator of thought and teaches all who enter ZOM the power of willed thought.

c. ANADISPI (Ah-nah-dee-ess-pee) teaches all who enter ZOM how consciousness linked with will can control things and events.

2. ARN

a. DOAGNIS (Doh-ah-geh-nee-seh) initiates all who enter ARN into the meaning of love and the illusion of names and labels.

b. PAKASNA (Pah-kah-ess-nah) initiates all who enter ARN into the meaning of love and the Eternal Feminine.

c. DIAIVOLA (Dee-ah-ee-voh-ee-ah) initiates all who enter ARN into spiritual reality and the doctrines of the Esoteric Tradition.

c. DIAIVOLA (Dee-ah-ee-voh-ee-ah) initiates all who enter ARN into spiritual reality and the doctrines of the Esoteric Tradition.

1. LIL
   a. OKKODON (Oh-keh-koh-doh-en) initiates all who enter LIL into the occult doctrine of the Eternal Return.
   b. PASKOMB (Pah-ess-koh-em-beh) initiates all who enter LIL into the joy and peace of divinity.
   c. VALGARS (Val-gar-ess) initiates all who enter LIL into the esoteric meaning of passive acceptance.

RELATIONSHIP OF THE AETHYRS
TO STANDARD UNIVERSE MODELS

The best known universe model is the Qabalistic Tree of Life. This is the standard model used in Western magic to depict the invisible worlds and pathways. Figure 32 shows a standard model of this Tree for easy reference. H.P. Blavatsky introduced the Eastern *Gupta-Vidya* model in her monumental work, *THE SECRET DOCTRINE*. Figure 33 shows a representation of her model in the form of a *planetary chain* (each planet was said to be part of a chain or ring from spirit to matter and back again). Figure 34 shows an interpretation of this model with appropriate pathways for the reader to study.

The student of magic should consider the Globes of the Gupta-Vidya Model as equivalent to the Sephiroths. The only real difference is that the eleventh Sephiroth, Daath, is shown in Figure 33 as two Globes (B and F).

The model in Figure 34 shows a flow of creative energy from divine Be-ness to physicality and then back to Be-ness again (Be-ness is equivalent to the Thatness of Vedanta and the Emptiness of Buddhism). The model shows Be-ness dividing itself into a tendency to differentiate and a complementary tendency to unify. These two tendencies give rise to a spiritualized form of mentation wherein divinity recognizes itself as being separate from something else. The desire for knowledge about this "something else" motivates manifestation into duality and matter. This ultimately results in the formation of the four Globes A through D. Each Globe is more limited and more material than the other. At Globe D the creative impulse reaches a culmination. Divinity, having looked outward towards the "something else" now seeks to look inward towards itself. This inward impulse results in the formation of Globes E through G.

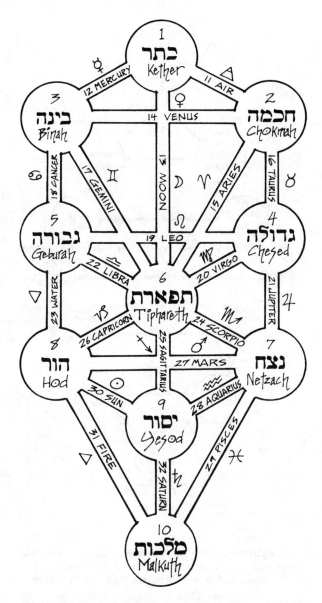

Figure 32. Typical Qabalistic Model, or Tree-of-Life.

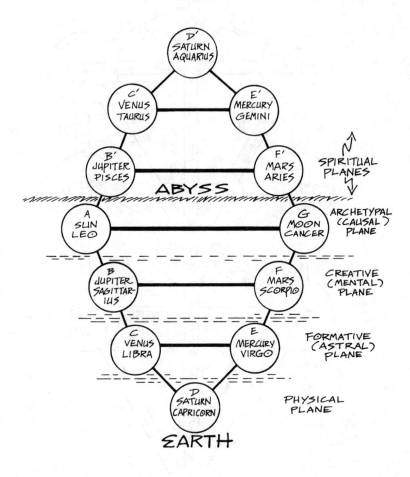

Figure 33. The Eastern Gupta-Vidya Model of the Earth Planetary Chain.
The planetary and astrological correspondences are from
the *Fountain-Source of Occultism* by G. de Purucker

(Theosophical University Press, Pasadena, CA)

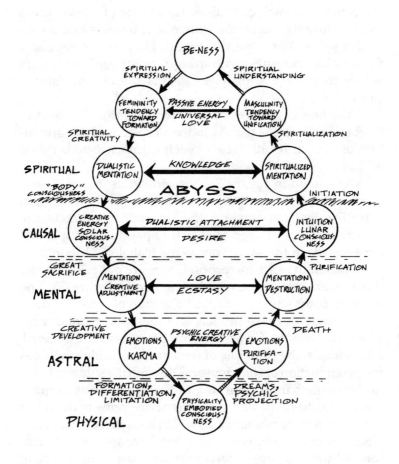

Figure 34. An interpretation of the Gupta-Vidya Model.

241

Simultaneously with the formation of each Globe, an expression of this same divine impulse appears in forms appropriate to each condition. These living forms express in miniature the same dualistic split of Be-ness into a subjective self and an objective world. They each comprise a focus of consciousness with an appropriate vehicle through which to acquire knowledge of this mysterious "something else".

The flow of manifestation downward from Globe A to Globe G represents the evolution of spirit and the involution of matter. A full circle of such manifestation is called a *Round*.

As shown in Figure 34, consciousness moves downward on the left side of the model and upward on the right side. The five cross-over paths are each two-directional. This model can be used to structure psychic and spiritual experiences in the same way as the Qabalistic Model.

Although exact correspondences are not possible, the Aethyrs are roughly situated as shown in Figure 35. The arrowed paths show the normal direction of consciousness.

A study of these models and their correspondences provides a wealth of insight into otherwise obscure material. For example, the principle of reincarnation which includes the peregrination of consciousness through the subtle spheres of the cosmos until returning to Earth, can be seen more clearly. In short, they serve as visual diagrams of the inner worlds and their relationships which are otherwise inaccessible to human comprehension. But there are dangers here too. All models have inherent limitations and make use of assumptions which color their output in some degree. Structures such as the Gupta-Vidya Model are double-edged. While enabling the mind to conceptualize the inconceivable, the mind can too easily take its own conceptualization as an objective fact. For example, it is tempting to believe that the seven cosmic planes are layered one

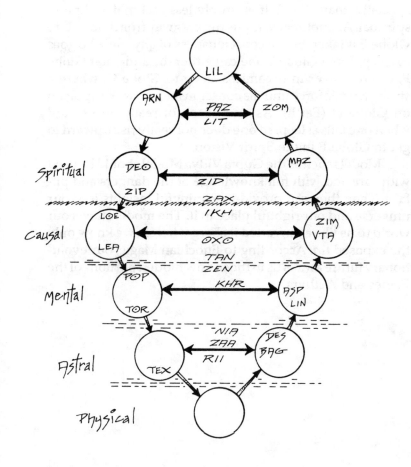

Figure 35. Relationship Between Aethyrs and Gupta-Vidya Models.

above the other, like steps on a ladder or the skins of an onion. Such is not the case. Kether is no more upward, spacially, than Yesod. It is simply less material and more spiritual. As another example, the pathway from Globe D to Globe E is taken by the consciousness of anyone who goes to sleep. From Globe E one can either die and enter Globe F, or cross over in dreamless sleep to Globe C, where a strong karmic force impells consciousness to wake up again on Globe D (Earth). As one does not really go upward when one falls asleep, so one does not really rise upward to get to Globe E in the Spirit Vision.

Models such as the Gupta Vidya Model should be used with care and with full knowledge of the dangers and pitfalls. Then they can provide meaningful insights into our universe and our rightful place in it. The model shows our world to be like an inverted iceberg wherein we know only the exposed tip. According to Enochian Magic, our evolutionary future awaits us in those now hidden portions of the Planes and Aethyrs.

APPENDIX A
ALEISTER CROWLEY'S VERSION OF
THE EIGHTEEN CALLS
As given in *Equinox Vol. I, No. 8,* since reprinted as
THE VISION AND THE VOICE (Samuel Weiser, N.Y.)

THE FIRST KEY
Ol sonuf vaoresaji, gohu IAD Balata, elanusaha caelazod: sobrazod-ol Roray i ta nazodapesad, Giraa ta maelpereji, das hoel-qo qaa notahoa zodimezod, od comemahe ta nobeloha zodien; soba tahil ginonupe pereje aladi, das vaurebes obolehe giresam. Casarem ohorela caba Pire: das zodonurenusagi cab: erem Iadanahe. Pilahe farezodem zodenurezoda adana gono Iadapiel das home-tohe: soba ipame lu ipamis: das sobolo vepe zodomeda poamal, od bogira aai ta piape Piamoel od Vaoan! Zodacare, eca, od zodameranu! odo cicale Qaa; zodoreje, lape zodiredo Noco Mada, Hoathahe I-A-I-D-A!

THE FIRST KEY
I reign over ye, saith the God of Justice, in power exalted above the Firmament of Wrath, in whose hands the Sun is as a sword, and the Moon as a through thrusting Fire: who measureth your Garments in the midst of my Vestures, and trussed you together as the palms of my hands. Whose seats I garnished with the Fire of Gathering, and beautified your garments with admiration. To whom I made a law to govern the Holy Ones, and delivered ye a Rod, with the Ark of Knowledge. Moreover you lifted up your voices and sware obedience and faith to Him that liveth and triumpheth: whose beginning is not, nor end cannot be: which shineth as a flame in the midst of your palaces, and reigneth amongst you as the balance of righteousness and truth!

Move therefore, and shew yourselves! Open the mysteries of your creation! Be friendly unto me, for I am the Servant of the same your God: the true worshipper of the of the Highest!

THE SECOND KEY

Adagita vau-pa-ahe zodonugonu fa-a-ipe salada! Vi-i-vau el! Sobame ial-pereji i-zoda-zodazod pi-adapehe ca-saarema aberameji ta ta-labo paracaleda qo-ta lores-el-qo turebesa ooge balatohe! Giui cahisa lusada oreri od mis-calapape cahisa bia ozodonugonu! lape noanu tarofe cor-esa tage o-quo maninu IA-I-DON. Torezodu! gohe-el, zodacare eca ca-no-quoda! zodmeranu micalazodo od ozodazodame vaurelar; lape zodir IOIAD!

THE SECOND KEY

Can the Wings of the Winds understand your voices of Wonder? O you! the second of the Firsts! whom the burning flames have framed in the depth of my Jaws! Whom I have pre-pared as cups for a wedding, or as the flowers in their beauty for the chamber of Righteousness! Stronger are your feet than the barren stone: and mightier are your voices than the mannds! For you are become a building such as is not, save in the Mind of the All-Powerful.

Arise, saith the First: Move therefore unto his servants! Shew yourselves in power, and make me a strong Seer-of-things: for I am of Him that liveth for ever!

THE THIRD KEY

Micama! goho Pe-IAD! zodir com-selahe azodien biabe os-lon-dohe. Norezoda cahisa otahila Gigipahe; vaunud-el-cahisa ta-pu-ime qo-mos-pelehe telocahe; qui-i-inu tol-toregi cahisa i cahisaji em ozodien; dasata beregida od torezodul! Ili e-Ol balazodareji, od aala tahilanu-os netaabe: daluga vaomesareji elonusa cape-mi-ali vaoresa *cala* homila; cocasabe fafenu izodizodope, od miinoagi de ginetaabe: vaunu na-na-e-el: panupire malapireji caosaji. Pilada naonu he balata od-vaoan. Do-o-i-ape mada: goholore, gohus, ami-ranu! Micama! Yehusozod ca-ca-com, od do-o-a-inu noari micaolazoda a-ai-om. Casaarameji gohia: Zodacare! Vaunigi-laji! od im-ua-mar pugo pelapeli Ananael Qo-a-an.

THE THIRD KEY

Behold! saith your God! I am a circle on whose hands stand twelve Kingdoms. Six are the seats of living breath: the rest are as sharp Sickles, or the Horns of Death. Wherein the creatures of Earth are and are not, except (in) mine own hands; which sleep and shall rise!

In the First I made ye stewards, and placed ye in twelve seats of government: giving unto every one of you power over the 456 true ages of time: that from the highest vessels and the corners of your governments you might work my Power, pouring down the fires of life and increase continually on earth. Thus you become the skirts of Justice and Truth.

In the name of the same your God, lift up, I say, yourselves!

Behold! His mercies flourish, and (His) Name is become mighty among us. In whom we say: Move! Descend! and apply yourselves unto us as unto the partakers of His Secret Wisdom in your Creation.

THE FOURTH KEY

Otahil elasadi babaje, od dorepaha gohol: gi-cahisaje auauago coremepe *peda*, dasonuf vi-vau-di-vau? Casaremi oeli *meapeme* sobame agi coremepo carep-el: casaremeji caro-o-dazodi cahisa od vaugeji; dasata ca-pi-mali cahisa ca-pi-ma-on: od elonusahinu cahisa ta el-o *calaa.* tore-zodu nor-quasahi od fe-caosaga: Bagile zodir e-na-IAD: das iod apila! Do-o-ipe quo-A-AL, zodacare! Zoda-meranu obeli-sonugi resat-el aaf nor-mo-lapi!

THE FOURTH KEY

I have set my feet in the South, and have looked about me, saying: are not the thunders of increase numbered 33, which reign in the second Angle?

Under who I have placed 9639: whom none hath yet numbered, but One; in whom the Second Beginnings of Things are and wax strong, which also successively are the Numbers of Time: and their powers are as the first 456.

Arise! you sons of Pleasure! and visit the earth: for I am the Lord your God; which is and liveth (for ever)! In the name of the Creator, move! and shew yourselves as pleasant deliverers, that you may praise Him among the sons of men!

THE FIFTH KEY

Sapahe zodimii du-i-be, od noasa ta qu-a-nis, adaro-cahe dorepehal caosagi od faonutas peripeso ta-be-liore. Casareme A-me-ipezodi na-zodaretahe *afa*; od dalugare zodizodope zodelida caosaji tol-toregi; od zod-cahisa esi-asacahe El ta-vi-vau; od iao-d tahilda das hubare *pe-o-al*; soba coremefa cahisa ta ela Vaulasa od Quo-Co-Casabe. Eca niisa od darebesa quo-a-asa: fetahe-ar-ezodi od beliora: ia-ial eda-nasa cicalesa; bagile Ge-iad I-el!

THE FIFTH KEY

The mighty sounds have entered into the third angle, and are become as olives in the Olive Mount; looking with gladness upon the earth, and dwelling in the brightness of the Heavens as continual Comforters.

Unto whom I fastened 19 Pillars of Gladness, and gave them vessels to water the earth with her creatures; and they are the brothers of the First and Second, and the beginning of their own seats, which are garnished with 69,636 ever-burning lamps: whose numbers are as the First, the Ends, and the Contents of Time.

Therefore come ye and obey your creation: visit us in peace and comfort: conclude us receivers of your mysteries: for why? Our Lord and Master is the All-One!

THE SIXTH KEY

Gahe sa-div cahisa *em*, micalazoda Pil-zodinu, sobam El haraji mir babalonu od obeloce samevelaji, dalagare mala-pereji ar-caosaji od *acame* canale, sobola zodare fa-beliareda caosaji od cahisa aneta-na miame ta Viv od Da. Daresare Sol-petahe-bienu Be-ri-ta od zodacame ji-mi-calazodo: sob-ha-atahe tarianu luia-he od ecarinu MADA Qu-a-a-on!

THE SIXTH KEY

The Spirits of the fourth angle are Nine Mighty in the Firmament of Waters: whom the First hath planted, a torment to the wicked and a garland to the righteous: giving unto them fiery darts to vanne the earth, and 7699 continual workmen, whose courses visit with comfort the earth; and are in government and continuance as the Second and the Third—

Therefore hearken unto my voice! I have talked of you, and I move you in power and presence, whose works shall be a song of honour, and the praise of your God in your Creation!

THE SEVENTH KEY

Ra-asa isalamanu para-di-zoda oe-cari-mi aao iala-pire-gahe Qui-inu. Enai butamonu od inoasa *ni* pa-ra-diala. Casaremeji ujeare cahirelanu, od zodonace lucifatianu, caresa ta vavale-zodirenu tol-hami. Soba lonudohe od nuame cahisa ta Da o Desa vo-ma-dea od pi-beliare itahila rita od miame ca-ni-quola rita! Zodacare! Zodameranu! Iecarimi Quo-a-dahe od I-mica-ol-zododa aaiome. Bajirele papenore idalugama elonusahi—od umapelifa vau-ge-ji Bijil—IAD!

THE SEVENTH KEY

The East is a house of Virgins singing praises among the flames of first glory wherein the Lord hath opened his mouth; and they are become 28 living dwellings in whom the strength of man rejoiceth; and they are apparelled with ornaments of brightness, such as work wonders on all creatures. Whose kingdoms and continuance are as the Third and Fourth, strong towers and places of comfort, the Seats of Mercy and Continuance. O ye Servants of Mercy, Move! Appear! Sing praises unto the Creator; and be mighty amongst us. For that to this remembrance is given power, and our strength waxeth strong in our Comforter!

THE EIGHTH KEY

Bazodemeo i ta pi-ripesonu olanu Na-zodavabebe *ox.*
Cassremeji varanu cahisa vaugeji asa berameji balatoha:
goho IAD. Soba miame tarianu ta lolacis Abaivoninu od
azodiajiere riore. Irejila cahisa da das pa-aox busada Caosago,
das cahisa od ipuranu telocahe cacureji o-isalamahe lonucaho
od Vovina carebafe? NIISO! bagile avavago gohon. NIISO!
bagile momao siaionu, od mabezoda IAD oi asa-momare
poilape. NIIASA! Zoda-meranu ciaosi caosago od belioresa
od coresi ta a beramiji.

THE EIGHTH KEY

The Midday, the first is as the third Heaven made of 26
Hyacinthine Pillars, in whom the Elders are become strong,
which I have prepared for mine own Righteousness, saith
the Lord: whose long continuance shall be as bucklers to
the Stooping Dragon, and like unto the harvest of a Widow.
How many are there which remain in the Glory of the
Earth, which are, and shall not see Death until the House fall
and the Dragon sink? Come away! for the Thunders (of
increase) have spoken. Come away! for the Crowns of the
Temple and the Robe of Him that is, was, and shall be,
crowned are divided! Come forth! Appear! to the terror of
the Earth, and to our comfort, and to the comfort of such as
are prepared.

THE NINTH KEY

Micaoli beranusaji perejela napeta ialapore, das barinu
efafaje *Pe* vaunupeho olani od obezoda, soba-ca upaahe
cahisa tatanu od tarananu balie, alare busada so-bolunu od
cahisa hoel-qo ca-no-quodi *cial.* Vaunesa aladonu mom
caosago ta iasa olalore ginai limelala. amema cahisa sobra
madarida zod cahisa! Ooa moanu cahisa avini darilapi
caosajinu: od butamoni pareme zodumebi canilu. Dazodisa
etahamezoda cahisa dao, od mireka ozodola cahisa pidiai

Colalala. Ul ci ninu a sobame ucime. Bajile? IAD
BALATOHE cahirelanu pare! NIISO! od upe ofafafe; bajile
a-cocasahe icoresaka a uniji beliore.

THE NINTH KEY

A mighty guard of Fire with two-edged swords flaming
(which have eight Vials of wrath for two times and a half,
whose wings are of wormwood and of the marrow of salt),
have set their feet in the West, and are measured with their
9996 ministers. These gather up the moss of the Earth as the
rich man doth his Treasure. Cursed are they whose iniquities they are! In their eyes are mill-stones greater than
the earth, and from their mouths run seas of blood. Their
heads are covered with diamonds, and upon their heads are
marble stones. Happy is he on whom they frown not. For
why? The Lord of Righteousness rejoiceth in them! Come
away, and not your Vials: for that the time is such as
requireth Comfort.

THE TENTH KEY

Coraxo cahisa coremepe, od belanusa Lucala azodia-
zodore paebe Soba iisononu cahisa uirequoe *ope* copehanu
od racalire maasi bajile caosagi; das yalaponu dosiji od
basajime; od ox ex dazodisa siatarisa od salaberoxa cynux-
ire faboanu. Vaunala cahisa conusata das *daox* cocasa ol
Oanio yore vohima ol jizodyazoda od eoresa cocasaji pelosi
molui das pajeipe, laraji same darolanu matorebe cocasaji
emena. el pataralaxa uyolaci matabe nomiji mononusa olora
jinayo anujelareda. Ohyo! ohyo! ohyo! ohyo! ohyo! ohyo!
noibe Ohyo! caosagonu! Bajile madarida i zodirope cahiso
darisapa! NIISO! caripe ipe nidali!

THE TENTH KEY

The Thunders of Judgment and Wrath are numbered
and are harboured in the North, in the likeness of an Oak

whose branches are 22 nests of lamentation and weeping laid up for the earth: which burn night and day, and vomit out the heads of scorpions and live Sulpher mingled with poison. These be the thunders that, 5678 times in the twenty-fourth part of a moment, roar with a hundred mighty earth-quakes and a thousand times as many surges, which rest not, neither know any time here. One rock bringeth forth a thousand, even as the heart of man doth his thoughts. Woe! Woe! Woe! Woe! Woe! Woe! Yea, Woe be to the Earth, for her iniquity is, was, and shall be great. Come away! but not your mighty sounds!

THE ELEVENTH KEY
Oxiayala holado, od zodirome *O* coraxo das zodiladare raasyo. Od vabezodire cameliaxa od bahala: NIISO! salamanu telocahe! Casaremanu hoel-qo, od tita zod cahisa soba cor-emefa i ga. NIISA! bagile aberameji nonucape. Zodacare eca od Zodameranu! odo cicale Qaa! Zodoreje, lape zodiredo Noco Mada, hoathahe I-A-I-D-A!

THE ELEVENTH KEY
The mighty Seat groaned, and there were five Thunders that flew into the East. And the Eagle spake and cried aloud: come away from the House of Death! And they gathered themselves together and became (those) of whom it is measured, and it is as They are, whose number is 31. Come away! For I have prepared (a place) for you. Move therefore, and shew yourselves! Unveil the mysteries of your Crea-tion. Be friendly unto me, for I am the servant of the same your God: the true worshipper of the Highest.

THE TWELFTH KEY
Nonuci dasonuf Babaje od cahisa *ob* hubaio tibibipe: alalare ataraahe od ef! Darix fafenu *mianu* ar Enayo ovof! Soba dooainu aai i VONUPEHE. Zodacare, gohusa, od

Zodameranu. Odo cicale Qaa! Zodoreje, lape zodiredo Noco Mada, hoathahe I-A-I-D-A!

THE TWELFTH KEY

O ye that range in the South and are the 28 Lanterns of Sorrow, bind up your girdles and visit us! bring down your train 3663 (servitors), that the Lord may be magnified, whose name amongst ye is Wrath. Move! I say, and shew yourselves! Unveil the mysteries of your Creation. Be friendly unto me, for I am the servant of the same your God, the true worshipper of the Highest.

THE THIRTEENTH KEY

Napeai Babajehe das berinu *vax* ooaona larinuji vonupehe doalime: conisa olalogi oresaha das cahisa afefa. Micama isaro Mada od Lonu-sahi-toxa, das ivaumeda aai Jirosabe. Zodacare od Zodameranu. Odo cicale Qaa! Zodoreje, lape zodiredo Noco Mada, hoathahe I-A-I-D-A-.

THE THIRTEENTH KEY

O ye Swords of the South, which have 42 eyes to stir up the wrath of Sin: making men drunken which are empty: Behold the Promise of God, and His Power, which is called amongst ye a bitter sting! Move and Appear! unveil the mysteries of your Creation, for I am the servant of the same your God, the true worshipper of the Highest.

THE FOURTEENTH KEY

Noroni bajihie pasahasa Oiada! das tarinuta mireca *ol* tahila dodasa tolahame caosago *h*omida: das berinu orocahe *quare:* Micama! Bial' Oiad; aisaro toxa das ivame aai Balatima. Zodacare od Zodameranu! Odo cicale Qaa! Zodoreje, lape zodiredo Noco Mada, hoathahe I-A-I-D-A.

THE FOURTEENTH KEY

O ye Sons of Fury, the Daughters of the Just One! that sit upon 24 seats, vexing all creatures of the Earth with age, that have 1636 under ye. Behold! The voice of God; the promise of Him who is called amongst ye Fury or Extreme Justice. Move and shew yourselves! Unveil the mysteries of your Creation; be friendly unto me, for I am the servant of the same your God: the true worshipper of the Highest!

THE FIFTEENTH KEY

Ilasa! tabaanu li-El pereta, casaremanu upaahi cahisa *dareji;* das oado caosaji oresacore: das omaxa monasaci Baeouibe od emetajisa Iaiadix. Zodacare od Zodameranu! Odo cicale Qaa. Zodoreje, lape zodiredo Noco Mada, hoathahe I-A-I-D-A.

THE FIFTEENTH KEY

O thou, the Governor of the first Flame, under whose wings are 6739; that weave the Earth with dryness: that knowest the Great Name "Righteousness," and the Seal of Honour. Move and Appear! Unveil the mysteries of your creation; be friendly unto me, for I am the servant of the same your God: the true worshipper of the Highest!

THE SIXTEENTH KEY

Ilasa viviala pereta! Salamanu balata, das acaro odazodi busada, od belioraxa balita: das inusi caosaji lusadanu *emoda*: das ome od taliobe: darilapa iehe ilasa Mada Zodil-odarepe. Zodacare od Zodameranu. Odo cicale Qaa: zodoreje, lape zodiredo Noco Mada, hoathahe I-A-I-D-A.

THE SIXTEENTH KEY

O thou second Flame, the House of Justice which hast thy beginning in glory and shalt comfort the Just: which walketh upon the Earth with 8763 feet, which understand

and separate creatures! Great art thou in the God of Stretch forth and Conquer. Move and appear! Unveil the mysteries of your Creation; be friendly unto me, for I am the servant of the same your God, the true worshipper of the Highest.

THE SEVENTEENTH KEY
Ilasa dial pereta! soba vaupaahe cahisa nanuba zodixalayo dodasihe od berinuta *faxisa* hubaro tasataxa yolasa: soba Iad *i* Vonupehe o Uonupehe: aladonu dax ila od toatare! Zodacare od Zodameranu! Odo cicale Qaa! Zodoreje, lape zodiredo Noco Mada, hoathahe I-A-I-D-A.

THE SEVENTEENTH KEY
O thou third Flame! whose wings are thorns to stir up vexation, and who hast 7336 living lamps going before Thee: whose God is "Wrath in Anger"—Gird up thy loins and hearken! Move and Appear! Unveil the mysteries of your Creation; be friendly unto me, for I am the servant of the same your God, the true worshipper of the Highest.

THE EIGHTEENTH KEY
Ilasa micalazoda olapireta ialpereji beliore: das odo Busadire Oiad ouoaresa caosago: casaremeji Laiada *eranu* berinutasa cafafame das ivemeda aqoso adoho Moz, od maoffasa. Bolape como belioreta pamebeta. Zodacare od Zodameranu! Odo cicale Qaa. Zodoreje, lape zodiredo Noco Mada, hoathahe I-A-I-D-A.

THE EIGHTEENTH KEY
O Thou might Light and burning Flame of Comfort! that unveilest the Glory of God to the centre of the Earth, in whom the 6332 secrets of Truth have their abiding, that is called in thy kingdom "Joy" and not to be measured.
Be thou a window of comfort unto me! Move and Appear! Unveil the mysteries of your Creation, be friendly unto me, for I am the servant of the same your God, the true worshipper of the highest.

thou a window of comfort unto me! Move and Appear! Unveil the mysteries of your Creation, be friendly unto me, for I am the servant of the same your God, the true worshipper of the highest.

ALEISTER CROWLEY'S VERSION OF THE CALL FOR THE AETHYRS

THE CALL OR KEY OF THE THIRTY AETHYRS

Madariatza das perifa LIL cahisa micaolazoda saanire caosago od fifisa balzodizodarasa Iaida. Nonuca gohulime: Micama adoianu MADA faoda beliorebe, soba ooaona cahisa luciftias peripesol, das aberaasasa nonucafe netaaibe caosaji od tilabe adapehaheta damepelozoda, tooata nonucafe jimicalazodoma larasada tofejilo marebe yareryo IDOIGO; od torezodulape yaodafe gohola, Caosaga, tabaoreda saanire, od caharisateosa yorepoila tiobela busadire, tilabe noalanu paida oresaba, od dodare-meni zodayolana. Elazodape tilaba paremeji peripesatza, od ta qurelesata booapisa. Lanibame oucaho sayomepe, od caharisateosa ajitoltorenu, mireca qo tiobela lela. Tonu paomebeda dizodalamo asa pianu, od caharisateosa aji-la-tore-torenu paracahe a sayomepe. Coredazodizoda dodapala od fifalazoda, lasa manada, od faregita bamesa omaoasa. Conisabera od auauotza tonuji oresa; catabela noasami tabejesa leuitahemonuji. Vanucahi omepetilabe oresa! Bagile? Moooabe OL coredazodizoda. el capimao itzomatzipe, od cacocasabe gosaa. Bajilenu pii tianuta a babalanuda, od faoregita teloca uo unime.

Madariiatza, torezodu!!! oadariatza orocaha aboaperi! Tabaori periazoda aretaabasa! Adarepanu coresata dobitza! Yolacame periazodi arecoazodiore, od quasabe qotinuji! ripire paaotzata sagacore! Umela od peredazodare cacareji Aoiveae coremepeta! Torezodu! zodacare od Zodameranu, asapeta sibesi butamona das surezodasa Tia balatanu. Odo cicale Qaa, od Ozodazodama pelapeli IADANAMADA!

THE CALL OR KEY OF
THE THIRTY AETHYRS

O ye Heavens which dwell in the First Aire, ye are mighty in the parts of the Earth, and execute the Judgment of the Highest! Unto you it is said: Behold the Face of your God, the beginning of comfort, whose eyes are the brightness of the Heavens, which provided you for the Government of the Earth, and her unspeakable variety, furnishing you with a power of understanding to dispose all things according to the Providence of Him that sitteth on the Holy Throne, and rose up in the Beginning, saying: The Earth, let her be governed by her parts, and let there be Division in her, that the glory of her may be always drunken, and vexed in itself. Her course, let it run with the Heavens; and as an handmaid let her serve them. One season, let it confound another, and let there be no creature upon or within her the same. All her members, let them differ in their qualities, and let there be no one Creature equal with another. The reasonable Creatures of the Earth, and Men, let them vex and weed out one another; and their dwelling-places, let them forget their Names. The work of man and his pomp, let them be defaced. His buildings, let them become Caves for the beasts of the Field! Confound her understanding with darkness! For why? it repenteth me that I have made Man. One while let her be known, and another while a stranger: because she is the bed of an Harlot, and the dwelling-place of him that is fallen.

O ye Heavens, arise! The lower heavens beneath you, let them serve you! Govern those that govern! Cast down such as fall. Bring forth with those that increase, and destroy the rotten. No place let it remain in one number. Add and diminish until the stars be numbered. Arise! Move! and appear before the covenant of His mouth, which He hath sworn unto us in His Justice. Open the Mysteries of your Creation, and make us partakers of THE UNDEFILED KNOWLEDGE.

APPENDIX C

AN ENOCHIAN DICTIONARY
Arranged by Gematric Value

Gematria No.	Enochian Word	Pronunciation	Meaning
1	–	–	–
2	–	–	–
3	F	eff	to visit
4	D	deh	one third
5	–	–	–
6	A	ah	I, my
7	–	–	–
8	G	geh	not, only
	L	el	first
9	T, TA	teh, tah	is, as, like, likeness, equality, equilibrium
	ZA	zodah	within
10	ATH	ah-teh	works
	ZAH	zodah	inside, inner
11	–	–	–
12	–	–	–
13	SA	sah	within
14	AG	ah-geh	no
15	AP	ah-peh	unchanging, same
	TA	tah	as
	GAH	gah	spirit, spirits
	ZA	zodah	within
16	ATH	ah-teh	works
	ZAH	zodah	inside, inner
17	ES	ess	one fourth, a quarter
18	AFFA	ah–ef–fah	empty
	EL	el	first
	GE	geh	not, only
	TAFA	tah–fah	poison
19	–	–	–
20	–	–	–
21	–	–	–
22	BALT	ball-teh	justice
23	–	–	–

Gematria No.	Enochian Word	Pronunciation	Meaning
24	TAFA	tah-fah	poison
25	ASPT	ah-seh-peh-teh	before, in front of
	BESZ	bess-zod	matter
	SALD	sal-deh	wonder
26	BAHAL	bah-hall	to shout, to yell, to cry
27	–	–	–
28	BALT	ball-teh	justice
29	–	–	–
30	ADPHAHT	ah-deh-peh-ah-teh	unspeakable
	PAEB	pah-eh-beh	oak
	PASHS	pah-seh-ess	children
31	ASPT	ah-seh-peh-teh	before, in front of
	BESZ	bess-zod	matter
32	–	–	–
33	PAGE	pah-geh	to rest
34	DO	doh	name
	TOH	toh	triumph
35	–	–	–
36	ADPHAHT	ah-deh-peh-ah-teh	unspeakable
	ELZAP	el-zodah-peh	way, course
37	–	–	–
38	OL	oh-el	to make, maker
39	HOL	hoh-el	to measure
	TABGES	tah-beh-gess	a cave
40	BABAGE	bah-bah-geh	South
	TOH	toh	triumph
41	EFAFAFE	eff-aff-aff-eh	vessels
	HOATH	hoh-ah-teh	true worshipper, devotee
	TOL	toh-el	all, everything
42	ELZAP	el-zodah-peh	way, course
43	–	–	–
44	OBZA	oh-beh-zodah	one half, dual
45	TABGES	tah-beh-gess	a cave
46	GLO	geh-loh	things
47	HOATH	hoh-ah-teh	a cave
	SOE	soh-eh	savior

Gematria No.	Enochian Word	Pronunciation	Meaning
	TOL	toh-el	all
48	ELO	el-oh	first
	TALHO	tah-leh-hoh	a cup
49	–	–	–
50	OBZA	oh-beh-zodah	one half, dual
51	GOSA	goh-sah	strange
52	QAA	quah-ah	creation
53	BALTOH	ball-toh	righteous
54	TALHO	tah-leh-hoh	cup
55	–	–	–
56	DODSEH	doh-dess-eh	vexation
57	GOSAA	goh-sah-ah	a stranger
58	BOGPA	boh-geh-pah	to govern
59	BALTOH	ball-toh	righteous
60	I	ee	is, is not
61	–	–	–
62	–	–	–
63	ZEN	zod-en	sacrifice
64	ODO	oh-doh	to open
65	BI	bee	voice
66	ADNA	ah-deh-nah	obedience
	IA	ee-ah	truth
	TOTO	toh-toh	cycles
67	–	–	–
68	IL	ee-el	Aethyr
69	GOHO	goh-hoh	to say, to speak
	IP	ee-peh	not
	ZEN	zod-en	sacrifice
70	IAD	ee-ah-doh	a god, God
	OADO	oh-ah-doh	to weave
71	BIA	bee-ah	voices
72	AAI	ah-ahee	within you
	FAFEn	eff-aff-en	to train
	THIL	the-hee-el	seat
	TOOAT	teh-oh-ah-teh	to provide
73	–	–	–
74	IAL	ee-all	to consume
75	NAZPS	nah-zod-pess	a sword
76	TABAAN	tah-bah-an	governor

Gematria No.	Enochian Word	Pronunciation	Meaning
77	ABAI	ah-ba-ee	stooping, to stoop down
	ED-NAS	ed-nah-ess	receivers
78	THIL	teh-hee-el	seat
	TOTO	toh-toh	cycles
79	HOLQ	hoh-el-que	are measured
	PAID	pah-ee-deh	always
80	DAZIS	dah-zodee-ess	head, heads
	NETAAB	neh-tah-ah-beh	government
81	NAPEA	nah-peh-ah	two-edged sword
	NAZPS	nah-zod-pess	sword
82	BALIT	bah-lee-teh	the just
	BUZD	buh-zod-deh	glory
	TABAAN	tah-bah-an	governor
83	FIFALZ	fee-fall-zod	to eliminate, to weed out
	ZON	zodoh-en	form
84	LAIAD	lah-ee-ah-deh	secrets of truth
	OLLOG	oh-el-loh-geh	men
	PIAP	pee-ah-peh	balance, scale
	TOOAT	toh-oh-ah-teh	to provide
85	VLS	fel-ess	the ends, farthest reaches
86	DAZIS	dah-zodee-ess	head
	NETAAB	neh-tah-ah-beh	government
87	–	–	–
88	BALIT	bah-lee-teh	the just
	BUZD	buh-zod-deh	glory
	GNETAAB	gen-etah-ah-beh	government, only government
89	APILA	ah-pee-lah	eternal life, to live forever
	BALIE	bah-lee-eh	salt
	FIFALZ	fee-fall-zod	to eliminate
	LUSD	luh-ess-deh	feet
	PON	poh-en	to destroy
	ZON	zod-en	form
90	BAGHIE	bah-geh-hee-eh	fury

Gematria No.	Enochian Word	Pronunciation	Meaning
	SONF	soh-en-eff	to reign
91	–	–	–
92	TOANT	toh-an-teh	love, union
	VPAAH	veh-pah-ah	wings
93	–	–	–
94	GNETAAB	geh-etah-ah-beh	govenrment
95	–	–	–
96	–	–	–
97	–	–	–
98	–	–	–
99	FAONTS	fah-oh-en-tess	to dwell in
	MAZ	mah-zod	appearance
100	FABOAN	fah-boh-an	poison
	IAOD	ee-ah-oh-deh	the beginning
	MAD	man-deh	god, your god
	OIAD	oh-ee-ah-deh	god, the just
	PLAPLI	peh-lah-peh-lee	users, partakers
101	LONSA	loh-en-sah	everyone
102	OTHIL	oh-teh-hee-el	seat
103	–	–	–
104	BAZM	bah-zod-em	noon, midday
	MAL	mah-el	arrow
	TOANT	toh-an-teh	love
105	FAONTS	fah-oh-en-tess	to dwell in
	MAZ	mah-zod	appearance
	PAM	pah-em	beginning
	ZIZOP	zodee-zodoh-pah	vessels
106	AR	are	the sun, to protect
	EOPHAN	eh-oh-peh-han	sorrow
107	–	–	–
108	BAMS	bah-mess	to forget
	OTHIL	oh-teh-hee-el	seat
109	DOSIG	doh-see-geh	night
	ZAR	zod-ar	ways, paths, courses
110	BABALON	bah-bah-loh-en	evil, wicked
	BASM	bah-zod-em	noon, midday
111	–	–	–
112	–	–	–

Gematria No.	Enochian Word	Pronunciation	Meaning
113	ZIN	zodee-en	waters
114	BABALOND	bah-bah-loh-en-deh	harlot, seductress
115	EOLIS	eh-oh-lee-ess	to make
	HARG	har-geh	to plant, to sow
	ZAR	sod-ar	ways, paths, courses
116	POILP	poh-ee-el-peh	to be divided
117	NANBA	nah-en-beh	thorns
	ZIZOP	zodee-zodoh-pah	vessels
118	GONO	goh-noh	faith
119	RAAS	rah-ah-seh	the East
	ZIN	zodee-en	waters
120	GRAA	geh-rah-ah	the Moon
	OM	oh-meh	to know, understand
121	HOM	hoh-meh	to live
122	DARBS	dar-bess	obedience
123	LONDOH	loh-en-doh	kingdoms
	MOZ	moh-zod	joy
124	GNAY	geh-nay	to do, does
125	LRASD	el-rah-ess-deh	to dispose of, to eliminate
126	OMA	oh-mah	understanding
127	IADNAH	ee-ah-deh-nah	knowledge
	PRGE	par-geh	fire
128	TIANTA	tee-an-en-tah	a bed
	QUASB	quah-seh-beh	to ruin, destroy
129	MOZ	moh-zod	joy
130	VNPH	ven-peh	anger
131	ETHAMZA	en-teh-ham-zodah	to be covered, hidden
132	–	–	–
133	OVOF	oh-voh-feh	to be magnified
134	–	–	–
135	–	–	–
136	ANANAEL	ah-nah-nah-el	the Secret Wisdom
	BALZARG	bal-zodah-rah-geh	stewards
	IAIDA	ee-ah-ee-dah	the highest
137	FISIS	fee-see-ess	to do, perform
	ORS	oh-ress	darkness
138	–	–	–
139	SIBSI	see-beh-see	covenant
140	TIANTA	tee-an-en-tah	a bed
141	–	–	–

Gematria No.	Enochian Word	Pronunciation	Meaning
142	BALZARG	bal-zodah-rah-geh	stewards
	TIBIBP	tee-bee-beh-peh	sorrow
143	ABRAASSA	ah-beh-rah-ah-ess-sah	to provide
	MOLAP	moh-lah-peh	men
144	–	–	–
145	NOIB	noh-ee-beh	yes, affirmation
146	–	–	–
147	BRGDO	bar-geh-doh	sleep
148	ORSBA	oh-ress-bah	drunken, intoxicated
	TIBIBP	tee-bee-beh-peh	sorrow
149	POAMAL	poh-ah-mal	palace
150	MI	mee	power
	OLPRT	oh-el-par-teh	light
151	ZORGE	zodah-ra-geh	love, friendly
152	GIGIPAH	gee-gee-pah	living breath
	OLLAR	oh-leh-lar	man
153	–	–	–
154	VAUL	vah-u-el	to work, toil
155	MOSPLEH	moh-seh-pel-eh-heh	horns
156	LONSHI	loh-en-ess-hee	power
	OLPRT	oh-el-par-teh	light
157	ZORGE	zodoh-ra-geh	love, friendly
158	NOQOL	noh-quo-leh	servants
159	–	–	–
160	IO-IAD	ee-oh-ee-ah-deh	Eternal God
161	–	–	–
162	VAOAN	vah-oh-ah-en	truth
163	QANIS	quah-nee-ess	olives
	RIT	ree-teh	mercy
164	–	–	–
165	–	–	–
166	–	–	–
167	SALMAN	sah-leh-mah-neh	a house
168	–	–	–
169	PIR	pee-ar	bright
	RIT	ree-teh	mercy
170	–	–	–
171	APOPHRASZ	ah-poh-peh-rah-seh-zod	motion

Gematria No.	Enochian Word	Pronunciation	Meaning
172	–	–	–
173	–	–	–
174	OLORA	oh-loh-rah	man
175	–	–	–
176	BASGIM	bah-seh-gee-em	day
177	APOPHRASZ	ah-poh-peh-rah-seh-zod	motion
	INSI	ee-ness-ee	to walk on, to tread
	NIIS	nee-ee-ess	to come
178	–	–	–
179	BLIAR	beh-lee-ah-rah	comfort, ease
180	LIMLAL	lee-em-lah-leh	treasure
181	ZILDAR	zodee-leh-dar	to fly
182	–	–	–
183	BLIARD	beh-lee-ah-rah-deh	to be with comfort
	ETHARZI	eh-teh-har-zodee	in peace
184	–	–	–
185	–	–	–
186	BAEQUIB	bah-eh-oh-u-ee-beh	righteousness
187	MOOOAH	moh-oh-oh-ah	it rejoices me
	ZILDAR	zodee-leh-dar	to fly
188	BITOM	bee-toh-em	fire
	VNIG	veh-nee-geh	to require, need
189	–	–	–
190	QUASAHI	quah-sah-hee	pleasure, delight
191	IALPRG	ee-al-par-geh	burning flames
192	AMMA	ah-em-mah	cursed
193	LORSLQ	loh-ress-el-que	flowers
194	BITOM	bee-toh-em	fire
	PARADIZ	pah-rah-dee-zod	a virgin
195	ETHARZI	eh-teh-har-zodee	in peace
196	DLUGAR	deh-lu-gar	to give
197	ISRO	ee-ess-roh	promise
	VRELP	var-el-peh	an adept, seer
198	BALZIZRAS	bal-zodee-zod-rass	judgment
	DOALIM	doh-ah-lee-em	sin
199	–	–	–
200	LIALPRT	lee-al-par-teh	the First Flame
210	BALZIZRAS	bal-zodee-zod-rass	judgment

APPENDIX D

THE EGYPTTIAN DEITIES AND SPHINXES: HOW TO USE THEM FOR SPIRIT VISION

The fifteen Egyptian deities associated with the Lesser Squares of the Watchtowers (see Table VIII on page 114) are shown in the accompanying figure. They are shown color coded in order to allow the student to make replicas. It is suggested that every student make his/her own replicas of the Watchtower pyramids, the deities and sphinxes out of cardboard or heavy paper and then paint them appropriately with tempra or any other suitable medium as follows:

1. Make the sides of the Watchtower pyramid. Construct sixteen triangles of equal size. Then cut the tops off to make truncated triangles. Paint four red, four yellow, four blue and four black.

2. Make the Egyptian sphinxes. Construct a red lion, a black bull, a blue eagle and a yellow angel. Make each Kerubic figure the same height and width. Cut each figure horizontally into three equal sections. Then cut the middle section horizontally in half to make four overall pieces each. By interchanging these sections, it will be possible to form replicas of any of the sphinxes.

3. Make the Watchtower pyramid. Construct one truncated pyramid. Make the four sides the same size as the triangles. Also, make the truncated top surface big enough to hold any sphinx and include a slot on it near the center for the god.

4. Make the Egyptian deities. Construct small figures of each of the fifteen deities as shown in the accompanying figure. Leave a small tongue at the bottom of each god. Each god-form can then be mounted onto the top face of the pyramid by inserting the tongue into the slot.

5. The pieces made in this way can be used by the student to simulate any of the Lesser Watchtower pyramids. Place the appropriate triangles on the sides of the pyramids, insert the god into the slot on the top surface, and place the sphinx on the top surface near the god. Use this simulation to aid in Spirit Vision by stimulating the magical imagination.

1.   2.   3.   4.

7.   6.   5.

Color Key

▦	Blue	▥	Orange	White and black
▧	Green	▥	Red	are as shown on
⋮	Yellow	▩	Purple	on the sketches.

8. 9. 10. 11.

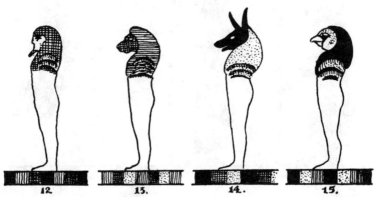

12. 13. 14. 15.

Orange head	Blue head	Black head.	White head with
Blue Nemyss	Orange Nemyss	Yellow Nemyss.	black & yellow.
Stripes: black,	Stripes: blue	Stripes: Blue,	Stripes; red,
orange & yellow.	& yellow.	yellow, & black.	yellow, & black.

STAY IN TOUCH

On the following pages you will find listed, with their current prices, some of the books now available on related subjects. Your book dealer stocks most of these and will stock new titles in the Llewellyn series as they become available. We urge your patronage.

TO GET A FREE CATALOG

Write for our monthly catalog, *Llewellyn's New Worlds of Mind and Spirit*. A sample copy is free, or you may subscribe for just $10 in the United States and Canada ($20 overseas, first class mail). Many bookstores also have *New Worlds* available to their customers. Ask for it.

In *New Worlds* you will find news and features about new books, tapes and services; announcements of meetings and seminars; helpful articles; author interviews and much more. Write to:

Llewellyn's New Worlds of Mind and Spirit
P.O. Box 64383, Dept. L710, St. Paul, MN 55164-0383, U.S.A.

TO ORDER BOOKS AND TAPES

If your book store does not carry the titles described on the following pages, you may order them directly from Llewellyn by sending the full price in U.S. funds, plus postage and handling (see below).

Credit Card Orders: VISA, Master Card, American Express are accepted. Call toll-free in the USA and Canada at 1-800-THE-MOON.

Special Group Discount: Because there is a great deal of interest in group discussion and study of the subject matter of this book, we offer a 20% quantity discount to group leaders or agents. Our Special Quantity Price for a minimum order of five copies of *Enochian Magic* is $51.80 cash-with-order. Include postage and handling charges noted below.

Postage and Handling: Include $4 postage and handling for orders $15 and under; $5 for orders *over* $15. There are no postage and handling charges for orders over $100. Postage and handling rates are subject to change. We ship UPS whenever possible within the continental United States; delivery is guaranteed. Please provide your street address as UPS does not deliver to P.O. boxes. Orders shipped to Alaska, Hawaii, Canada, Mexico and Puerto Rico will be sent via first class mail. Allow 4-6 weeks for delivery. **International orders:** Airmail – add retail price of each book and $5 for each non-book item (audiotapes, etc.); Surface mail – add $1 per item. Minnesota residents please add 7% sales tax.

Mail orders to:
Llewellyn Worldwide
P.O. Box 64383, Dept. L710, St. Paul, MN 55164-0383, U.S.A.
For customer service call 1-800-THE-MOON
In Minnesota, call (612) 291-1970

Prices subject to change without notice.

THE ENOCHIAN TAROT DECK
Created by Gerald and Betty Schueler
Painted by Sallie Ann Glassman

The Enochian Tarot is a deck of cards which is primarily used to foretell the future. Forecasting the future, however, is only a superficial use of the massive powers of the Enochian Tarot. Here is a powerful tool which allows you to look deep inside your subconscious and "see" the direction your life is taking. The Enochian Tarot is an easy-to-use system of self-discovery which allows you to see your relationship to God and the universe.

The Enochian Tarot Deck consists of 86 cards divided into two sections: a Major Arcana and a Minor Arcana. The Major Arcana is a set of 30 picture cards which are also called The Greater Arcana, Trumps, Atouts, or Triumphs. These cards are symbolic representations of various cosmic forces such as Doubt, Intuition, Glory, etc. The Minor Arcana contains 56 cards which represent the Four Enochian Watchtowers. The Minor Arcana is divided into four suits called Earth, Water, Air, and Fire.

0-87542-708-1, boxed set: 86 cards with booklet $12.95

THE ENOCHIAN MAGICK OF DR. JOHN DEE
Geoffrey James

Dee's system of Enochian Magick is among the most powerful in the Western tradition. This book has become an occult classic because it holds all the secrets of Dee's private magical workbooks, as recorded in the late sixteenth century.

This treasure of Enochian lore offers the only definitive version of the famous Angelical Calls or Keys, conjurations said to summon the angels of the heavenly sphere—as well as all the practical information necessary for the experienced magician to reproduce Dee's occult experiments, with details on how to generate the names of the angels, create Enochian talismans, and set up an Enochian temple. This version of Dee's system of planetary and elemental magic offers material sure to fascinate a new generation of students of Enochian Magick. Explore the source texts that inspired MacGregor Mathers, Aleister Crowley, Israel Regardie, and a host of others and learn to practice angelic magick!

1–56718–367–0, 6 x 9, 248 pp., illus. $14.95

TETRAGRAMMATON
The Secret to Evoking Angelic Powers and the Key to the Apocalypse
Donald Tyson

In Western magick, "Tetragrammaton" is the holiest name of God. It is composed of the four Hebrew letters IHVH and is the occult key that unlocks the meaning behind astrological symbolism, the tarot, the mysteries of the Old Testament and the Book of Revelation, the kabbalah, the Enochian magick of John Dee, and modern ritual magick. It is nothing less than the archetypal blueprint of creation, the basis for such fundamental forms as the DNA double helix and the binary language of modern computers. Its true structure is the great arcanum of occultism, which has never before been explicitly revealed but only hinted at in obscure religious and alchemical emblems. Now, for the first time, its true structure is laid bare in a clear and unambiguous manner, allowing this potent key to open astounding vistas of understanding.

1-56718-744-7, 320 pp., 7 x 10, softcover $24.95

PLANETARY MAGICK
A Complete System for Knowledge and Attainment
Denning & Phillips

Invoke and direct the Powers of the Planets . . . for psycho-spiritual wholeness, development of creative magickal power, exploration of the Inner Planes, evocation of spirits, and material prosperity

Planetary Magick lies at the root of all astrological, alchemical and Qabalistic lore. Although the planetary powers of the cosmos are far beyond our intervention, their counterparts in the depths of the psyche are within our reach by certain special meditative and ritual methods. The complete system of Planetary Magick is set forth here, and is designed for both the newcomer and the established mage. This book includes 65 never-before-published magickal rites in full detail, and provides you with a thorough understanding of the essential practical heart of Western Magick.

0-87542-193-8, 456 pp., 6 x 9, illus., softcover $15.00

Prices subject to change without notice.

THE GOLDEN DAWN
The Original Account of the Teachings, Rites & Ceremonies of the Hermetic Order
As revealed by Israel Regardie

Complete in one volume with further revision, expansion, and additional notes by Regardie, Cris Monnastre, and others. Expanded with an index of more than 100 pages! Also included are Initiation Ceremonies, important rituals for consecration and invocation, methods of meditation and magical working based on the Enochian Tablets, studies in the Tarot, and the system of Qabalistic Correspondences that unite the World's religions and magical traditions into a comprehensive and practical whole.

This volume is designed as a study and practice curriculum. Meditation upon, and following with the Active Imagination, the Initiation Ceremonies are fully experiential without need of participation in group or lodge. A very complete reference encyclopedia of Western Magick.

0–87542–663–8, 840 pp., 6 x 9, illus., softcover $24.95

GOLDEN DAWN ENOCHIAN MAGIC
Pat Zalewski

Enochian magic is considered by most magicians to be the most powerful system. Aleister Crowley learned this system of magic from the Hermetic Order of the Golden Dawn, which had developed and expanded the concepts and discoveries of Elizabethan magus John Dee. This book begins where the published versions of the Enochian material of the Golden Dawn leave off.

Based on the research and unpublished papers of MacGregor Mathers, one of the founders of the Golden Dawn, *Golden Dawn Enochian Magic* opens new avenues of use for this system. New insights are given on such topics as the Sigillum Dei Aemeth, the Angels of the Enochian Aires applied to the 12 tribes of Israel and the Kabbalah, the 91 Governors, the Elemental Tablets as applied to the celestial sphere, and more. This book provides a long-sought break from amateurish and inaccurate books on the subject; it is designed to complement such scholarly classics as *Enochian Invocation* and *Heptarchia Mystica*.

0–87542–898–3, 224 pp., 6 x 9, illus., softcover $14.95

Prices subject to change without notice.

MODERN MAGICK
Eleven Lessons in the High Magickal Arts
Donald Michael Kraig

Modern Magick is the most comprehensive step-by-step introduction to the art of ceremonial magic ever offered. The eleven lessons in this book will guide you from the easiest of rituals and the construction of your magickal tools through the highest forms of magick: designing your own rituals and doing pathworking. Along the way you will learn the secrets of the Kabbalah in a clear and easy-to-understand manner. You will discover the true secrets of invocation (channeling) and evocation, and the missing information that will finally make the ancient grimoires, such as the "Keys of Solomon," not only comprehensible, but usable. This book also contains one of the most in-depth chapters on sex magick ever written. *Modern Magick* is designed so anyone can use it, and it is the perfect guidebook for students and classes. It will also help to round out the knowledge of long-time practitioners of the magickal arts.

  0–87542–324–8, 592 pp., 6 x 9, illus., index, softcover $17.95

GODWIN'S CABALISTIC ENCYCLOPEDIA
Complete Guidance to Both Practical and Esoteric Applications
David Godwin

One of the most valuable books on the Cabala is back, with a new and more usable format. All entries, which had been scattered throughout the appendices, are now incorporated into one comprehensive dictionary. There are hundreds of new entries and illustrations, making this book even more valuable for Cabalistic pathworking and meditation. It now has many new Hebrew words and names, as well as the terms of Freemasonry, the entities of the Cthulhu mythos, and the Aurum Solis spellings for the names of the demons of the Goetia. It contains authentic Hebrew spellings, and a new introduction that explains the uses of the book for meditation on God names.

The Cabalistic schema is native to the human psyche, and *Godwin's Cabalistic Encyclopedia* will be a valuable reference tool for all Cabalists, magicians, scholars and scientists of all disciplines.
1–56718–324–7, 832 pp., 6 x 9, softcover $24.95

Prices subject to change without notice.

AN ADVANCED GUIDE TO ENOCHIAN MAGICK
A Complete Manual of Angelic Magick
Gerald J. Schueler

This is a sequel to *Enochian Magic: A Practical Manual.* In this book, Schueler provides everything for the serious practitioner of the Enochian system. All students of the Golden Dawn, Aurum Solis and other mainstream systems of Western practice will find this work a practical "working manual" combining theory with exercises, complete rituals and outlines for multilevel magical operations. New students will find the Enochian system particularly modern, reflective of the new physics; others will be attracted to the feeling of working at the frontiers of the New Age.

The book includes information on Enochian Magick, Enochian Meditation, and Enochian Healing. It is an ideal book for beginning, intermediate or advanced students of magick and a vital resource and guidebook for occult Orders and Lodges.

0-87542-711-1, 448 pp., 5¼ x 8, illus., softcover   **$12.95**

EGYPTIAN MAGICK
Enter the Body of Light & Travel the Magickal Universe
Gerald & Betty Schueler

(Formerly *Coming Into the Light.*) The ancient Egyptians taught a complex philosophy which rivals the magickal doctrine taught today. Clearly documented is a major element of the system, the Magickal Universe—the invisible realm that exists all around us hidden from our physical senses. Through rituals, the Egyptian magician would enter his Body of Light, or auric body, and shift his consciousness; he could then see and converse with the gods, goddesses and other beings who are found in these regions.

This book reveals Egyptian magick in a way that has never been done before. It provides modern translations of the famous magickal texts known as *The Book of the Dead,* and shows that they are not simply religious prayers or spells to be spoken over the body of a dead king. Rather, they are powerful and highly effective rituals to be performed by living magicians who seek to know the truth about themselves and their world.

1-56718-604-1, 432 pp., 6 x 9, 24 color plates, softcover   **$19.95**

Prices subject to change without notice.

THE ENOCHIAN WORKBOOK
The Enochian Magickal System Presented in 43 Easy Lessons
Gerald J. and Betty Schueler

Enochian Magic is an extremely powerful and complex path to spiritual enlightenment. Here, at last, is the first book on the subject written specifically for the beginning student. Ideally suited for those who have tried other books on Enochia and found them to be too difficult, *The Enochian Workbook* presents the basic teachings of Enochian Magic in an easy-to-use workbook.

The authors have employed the latest techniques in educational psychology to help students master the information in this book. The book is comprised of 11 sections, containing a total of 43 lessons, with test questions following each section so students can gauge their progress. You will learn how to conduct selected rituals, skry using a crystal, and use the Enochian Tarot as a focus for productive meditation. Also explore Enochian Chess, Enochian Physics, and the dangers associated with Enochian Magic.

0-87542-719-7, 360 pp., 7 x 10, illus., 16 color plates $19.95

THE MAGICAL PHILOSOPHY, VOLUME 3
Mysteria Magica
Denning & Phillips

For years, Denning and Phillips headed the international occult Order Aurum Solis. In this book, they present the magickal system of the order so that you can use it. Here you will find rituals for banishing and invoking plus instructions for proper posture and breathing. You will learn astral projection, rising on the planes, and the magickal works that should be undertaken through astral projection. You will learn the basic principle of ceremonies and how to make sigils and talismans. You will learn practical Enochian magick plus how to create, consecrate and use your magickal tools such as the magickal sword, wand and cup.

Filled with illustrations, this book is an expanded version of the previous edition. It is now complete in itself and can be the basis of an entire magickal system. You can use the information alone or as the source book for a group. If you want to learn how to do real magick, this is the place you should start.

0-87542-196-2, 480 pp., 6 x 9, illus., softcover $15.00

Prices subject to change without notice.

THE ANGELS' MESSAGE TO HUMANITY
Ascension to Divine Union Powerful Enochian Magick
Gerald and Betty Schueler

Initiate yourself into one of the most enriching and powerful systems of magic anywhere. *The Angels' Message to Humanity* presents a radical, new system of 88 graded paths based on mandalas created from the five Enochian tablets. Incorporating ritual magic, visualization, yoga, and mantras, nothing apart from this book is needed for these initiations. The revised pathworking rituals in *The Angels' Message to Humanity* allow a magician to fully explore the Enochian system of magick, alone or with others.

Geared to the intermediate to advanced magical student, this book is divided into easy-to-read text and endnotes containing helpful references and technical information, as well as 121 illustrations and eight color plates. Explore the world of modern Enochian magick today!

1-56718-605-X, 352 pp., 7 x 10, illus., softcover $24.95

ANGEL MAGIC
The Ancient Art of Summoning & Communicating with Angelic Beings
Geoffrey James

One of the most universal religious beliefs is that a magician can harness the power of spiritual beings to gain influence and power over the physical world. The highest and most beautiful manifestation of this belief is Angel Magic, the art and science of communication with spiritual beings. Angel Magic is a set of ritual practices that is believed to control angels, daimons, fayries, genies, and other personifications of the elements, the planets, and the stars. Banned for centuries, it is at once the most practical and effective of the occult sciences. This book traces Angel Magic from its birth in folk magic and shamanism through centuries of oppression to its greatest flowering in works of the great magi of the Renaissance. You will learn how this system of magic was almost lost until the researchers of magical lodges saved it from obscurity. What's more, you will witness accounts of the modern day practice of this curious and powerful art.

1-56178-368-9, 224 pp., 6 x 9, illus., softcover $12.95

SELF-INITIATION INTO THE GOLDEN DAWN TRADITION
A Complete Curriculum of Study for Both the Solitary Magician and the Working Magical Group
Chic Cicero and Sandra Tabatha Cicero

Self-Initiation into the Golden Dawn Tradition offers self-paced instruction by the established authorities on this magical order! Without massive amounts of complex information, Golden Dawn experts Sandra Tabatha Cicero and Chic Cicero present direction that's clear and easy-to-follow. Upon completion of this workbook, you can be a practicing Golden Dawn magician with knowledge of Qabalah, astrology, tarot, geomancy and spiritual alchemy. Other than a desire to learn, there is no prerequisite for mastering this highly sought-after magical curriculum. Lessons in *Self-Initiation into the Golden Dawn Tradition* are enhanced by written examinations, daily rituals and meditative work. Become a Golden Dawn magician—without group membership or prohibitive expense—through the most complete, comprehensive and scientific system on Golden Dawn study to date!

1–56718–136–8, 800 pp., 7 x 10, softcover $39.95

SECRETS OF A GOLDEN DAWN TEMPLE
Chic Cicero and Sandra Tabatha Cicero

From its inception 100 years ago, the Hermetic Order of the Golden Dawn continues to be *the* authority on high magick. Yet the books written on the Golden Dawn system have fallen far short in explaining how to construct the tools and implements necessary for ritual. Until now.

This is the first book to describe *all* Golden Dawn implements and tools in complete detail. Here is a unique compilation of the various tools used, all described in full: wands, ritual clothing, elemental tools, Enochian tablets, altars, temple furniture, banners, lamens, admission badges and much more. This book provides instructions for the construction of nearly 80 different implements, all displayed in photographs or drawings. Plus, it gives a ritual or meditation for every magickal instrument presented. It truly is an indispensable guide for any student of Western Magickal Tradition.

0–87542–150–4, 592 pp., 6 x 9, 16 color plates, softcover $19.95

WESTERN MANDALAS OF TRANSFORMATION
Magical Squares • Tattwas • Qabalistic Talismans
Soror A.L.

Western Mandalas of Transformation reveals the uses of astrological and Qabalistic talismans for your spiritual use. Now you can learn the mysteries hidden in the ancient system of magical squares—some of which have never been published in the Western Magical Tradition!

This complete guide contains special sections on the meaning of numbers, planetary attributes, and sound and color healing. You get explanations of the secret techniques for awakening these images in your subconscious to energize your chakra system and personal aura. There is also a section on gematria for the seasoned Qabalist, and a full chapter on Daath and Pluto. Instruction in *Western Mandalas of Transformation* clears up mistakes and "blinds" in many other talismanic books of this century and is accompanied by more than 150 illustrations for your ease of learning.

1-56718-170-8, 7 x 10, 272 pp., color plates, softcover $19.95

THE TAO AND THE TREE OF LIFE
Alchemical and Sexual Mysteries of the East and West
Eric Yudelove

Until 1981, Taoist Yoga, or Taoist Internal Alchemy, remained a secret to the Western World. All of that changed when Master Mantak Chia emigrated from Thailand to the United States and began practicing openly. The complete Taoist Yoga system is now revealed—by one of Master Chia's first American students—in *The Tao and The Tree of Life.* Going beyond any previously published work, this book describes the entire structure of Taoist Yoga by comparing it with the Western Tradition of the Kaballah.

The Taoists developed the potential of human sexuality to a higher level than any other group. Beginners can benefit almost immediately from the practical exercises in *The Tao and the Tree of Life.* Seasoned Kabbalists will marvel at actual alchemical formulas uncovered from *The Sepher Yetzirah.*

1-56718-250-X, 256 pp., 5¼ x 8, illus., softcover $14.95

Prices subject to change without notice.